Common Core
Standards Practice Workbook

Grade 6

Teacher Guide

Glenview, Illinois • Boston, Massachusetts
Chandler, Arizona • Upper Saddle River, New Jersey

ALWAYS LEARNING

PEARSON

Pearson, Scott Foresman, Pearson Scott Foresman, and enVisionMATH are trademarks in the U.S. and/or in other countries, of Pearson Education Inc., or its affiliates.

ISBN-13: 978-0-328-75696-4
ISBN-10:   0-328-75696-2

3 4 5 6 7 8 9 10 V031 19 18 17 16 15 14

Grade 6 Contents

Standards Practice

Assessment

Teacher Support

About this Guide

Pearson is pleased to offer this **Common Core Standards Practice** Teacher's Guide, a companion to the **Common Core Standards Practice Workbook.** It includes these pages:

- **Common Core Standards Practice pages.** Two pages of practice exercises for each Common Core State Standard. Students will find different kinds of exercises that are similar to the items expected to be on the Next Generation Assessment that students will be taking starting in 2014–2015.

- **Practice for the Common Core Assessment.** Each Practice Assessment consists of one (1) Practice End-of-Year Assessment and two (2) Performance Tasks. One Practice Assessment is found in the Student Workbook, while the second is a "secure" test found only in this Teacher's Guide. The two Practice End-of-Year Assessments are mirror assessments.

  The Practice End-of-Year assessment was built to align to the content emphases of both PARCC and SBAC. That means that 70% of the items assess major content emphases. In addition, many of the items are similar to the innovative items that are expected to be on the upcoming Next Generation Assessments. Students will encounter multiple-response selected-response items; simulated technology-enabled items that ask students to sort answer options into appropriate categories or to construct responses on grids, graphs, and number lines; constructed response items that ask them to explain their reasoning or justify their thinking; and extended constructed response items that include multi-part questions with multi-step solutions. The Performance Tasks present students with problem situations in real-world context and ask students to make use of their developing proficiency with the Standards for Mathematical Practice and their firmer understanding of Math Content to find solutions.

- Answers to all of the student pages as 4-ups.

- **Correlation Chart for the Practice EOY Assessment.** The chart indicates for each item the Content Standard assessed and lessons in *enVisionMATH™ Common Core* and sessions in *Investigations in Number, Data, and Space® for the Common Core* where students can go for more practice of the standard assessed.

- **Scoring Rubrics for the four (4) Performance Tasks.** In additional to recommendations for scoring, these pages list both the Standards for Mathematical Practice and Mathematical Content that the task assesses.

Common Core Standards Practice and Assessments

Name _____

Common Core Standards Practice

6.RP.A.1 Understand the concept of a ratio and use ratio language to describe a ratio relationship between two quantities.

1. The table shows the number and type of bagels ordered for a breakfast meeting.

Type of Bagel	Number Ordered
Plain	12
Wheat	18
Blueberry	10

   a. The ratio of plain bagels to wheat bagels is 2:3. Does this ratio represent a part-to-part or a part-to-whole ratio? Explain your answer.

   b. The ratio of blueberry bagels to all bagels is 1:4. Does this ratio represent a part-to-part or a part-to-whole ratio? Explain your answer.

2. Melinda will be going to a new school in August. Her mother tells her that the student-teacher ratio at her new school is 18 to 1.

   a. Explain to Melinda what that ratio means.

   b. Should Melinda expect to have exactly 17 classmates in her new class? Explain you reasoning.

   c. In her new homeroom, Melinda counts 10 boys and 14 girls (including herself). What is the ratio of girls to boys in her new homeroom? Express the ratio in two different ways.

3. The table shows the kinds of muffins and the number sold by a bakery on a given day.

Kinds of Muffin	Number Sold
Cinnamon	15
Blueberry	20
Apple	10

a. Write a ratio that represents a part-to-part relationship. Explain the ratio.

b. Write a ratio that represents a part-to-whole relationship. Explain the ratio.

4. Badri is making orange juice from concentrate for breakfast. One can of concentrate is mixed with 3 cans of water. One can is equal to one cup.

a. Which ratio represents the relationship between concentrate and water?

A 1:3 **B** 3:1 **C** 3:4 **D** 1:4

b. Badri has a container that holds 2 quarts. Can he mix two cans of concentrate and water in the container? Explain your answer.

5. The students at Fields School have been asked to vote on new school hours. The two options are from 7:30 A.M. to 2:30 P.M. or from 8:15 A.M. to 3:15 P.M. The later start time won by a ratio of 2 to 1.

a. Explain what the ratio 2 to 1 means in this context.

b. If 300 students voted, how many voted for the earlier start time?

Name _____

Common Core Standards Practice

6.RP.A.2 Understand the concept of a unit rate $\frac{a}{b}$ associated with a ratio $a:b$ with $b \neq 0$, and use rate language in the context of a ratio relationship.

1. Trevor rode his bicycle 25 miles in 2 hours. Assuming Trevor rode at a constant speed, how many miles did Trevor ride in one hour?

   A 4 miles

   B 5 miles

   C 10 miles

   D $12\frac{1}{2}$ miles

2. A model dough recipe calls for 2 cups of salt, 1 cup of flour, and 2 cups of hot water. How many cups of flour are needed for each cup of salt?

   A $\frac{1}{2}$ cup of flour

   B 1 cup of flour

   C $1\frac{1}{2}$ cups of flour

   D 2 cups of flour

3. Dong Joon and Ella have set up 180 chairs at 15 tables for the spring sports banquet. They put the same number of chairs at each table.

   a. How many chairs did they put at each table?

   b. Write a ratio to represent the relationship between the tables and chairs.

4. Which of these ratios are rates? Circle all of the rates. Then find the unit rate for each rate.

   10 girls and 15 boys in a class

   300 miles driven and 15 gallons used

   4 energy bars for $10

   21 miles biked in one hour and a half

   20 pine trees to 30 maple trees

CC3

5. A banana bread recipe calls for 4 cups of flour, 2 cups of mashed banana, and 1 cup of sugar. How many cups of flour are needed for every cup of banana?

A 4 cups

B 3 cups

C 2 cups

D 1 cup

6. Mr. Hingle drove his car 300 miles on 12 gallons of gasoline. How many miles per gallon did Mr. Hingle's car get?

A 15 miles per gallon

B 20 miles per gallon

C 25 miles per gallon

D 3,600 miles per gallon

7. Dennis and his mother went to the farmer's market to buy fruits and vegetables. The table shows what they bought at the market.

Fruit and Vegetables	Cost
Squash (3 lb)	$2.97
Tomatoes (4 lb)	$11.96
Spinach ($1\frac{1}{2}$ lb)	$2.25
Turnips (2 lb)	$6.50
Strawberries (3 lb)	$9.75
Blueberries (2 lb)	$7.50

a. Find the unit rate for all of the fruits and vegetables that Dennis and his mother bought.

b. Which fruit or vegetable had the highest unit rate? Which had the lowest?

c. Can the units rates of all of the fruits and vegetables be compared? Explain.

Name _____

Common Core Standards Practice

6.RP.A.3a Use ratio and rate reasoning to solve real-world and mathematical problems, e.g., by reasoning about tables of equivalent ratios, tape diagrams, double number line diagrams, or equations. Make tables of equivalent ratios relating quantities with whole-number measurements, find missing values in the tables, and plot the pairs of values on the coordinate plane. Use tables to compare ratios.

1. Complete the table.

Feet	1			5	10	
Inches		24	36			144

2. The double number line below shows how many miles Renee biked on Sunday.

How many miles did she bike each hour?

3. Ama's mother makes tablecloths to sell. She just bought 36 yards of material that she will use to make 12 tablecloths.

a. Complete a table to show how much material Ama's mother needs to make different numbers of tablecloths.

Tablecloths	2	4	6	8	10	12	14
Yards of Material						36	

b. Plot the values on the coordinate grid below.

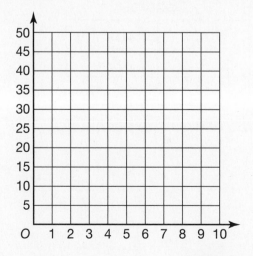

4. The table compares feet to yards.

a. Complete the table.

Feet	Yards
3	
6	
	3

b. Plot these values as ordered pairs on the coordinate grid.

c. How many yards equals 27 feet?

5. The two tables below show how much DeShawn and Sandra earn, depending upon the number of hours each works.

a. Complete the tables.

DeShawn		Sandra	
Hours	Earns ($)	Hours	Earns ($)
1		1	
7	85.75	8	92.80

b. Compare their rates of pay. Who earns more per hour?

Name _____

Common Core Standards Practice

6.RP.A.3b Use ratio and rate reasoning to solve real-world and mathematical problems, e.g., by reasoning about tables of equivalent ratios, tape diagrams, double number line diagrams, or equations. Solve unit rate problems including those involving unit pricing and constant speed.

1. The table shows the prices of 3 boxes of laundry detergent of different sizes. Which size box costs the least per ounce? Explain your answer.

Size	Price
150 oz	$18.97
100 oz	$11.97
56 oz	$8.97

2. Dora and her family are driving to visit relatives. They travel 174 miles in 3 hours.

   Assuming that they are traveling at a constant speed, how many miles do they travel in one hour?

3. It took Trinh 4 hours to ride her bicycle 48 miles. Assuming she rode at a constant speed, how many miles did she ride per hour?

4. Jana is going to pay $140 for 28 gymnastics lessons. Anil will pay $30 for 5 lessons.

   a. What is the rate per lesson for each?

   b. Who is paying more per lesson? How much more?

5. Mr. Vega is comparing the prices, shown in the table below, of 3 different jars of peanut butter. Which is the best buy? Explain.

Size	Price
18 oz	$3.28
28 oz	$4.73
40 oz	$6.44

6. A passenger train can travel 156 miles in 3 hours. Assuming that the train travels at a constant speed, how fast does the train travel per hour?

7. It took Rosa 7 hours to rake 3 lawns. Assuming that the lawns are all about the same size, about how long does it take Rosa to rake one lawn?

8. Chi is going to pay $132 for 12 guitar lessons. Kele will pay $78 for 6 lessons.

   a. What is the rate per lesson for each?

   b. Who is paying more per lesson? How much more?

Name _____

Common Core Standards Practice

6.RP.A.3c Use ratio and rate reasoning to solve real-world and mathematical problems, e.g., by reasoning about tables of equivalent ratios, tape diagrams, double number line diagrams, or equations. Find a percent of a quantity as a rate per 100 (e.g., 30% of a quantity means $\frac{30}{100}$ times the quantity); solve problems involving finding the whole, given a part and the percent.

1. During a 30% off sale, Lourdes pays $140 for a swing set. What was the original price of the swing set?

   A $42.00

   B $182.00

   C $200.00

   D $466.67

2. The Hoboken Renegades won 40% of their 180 games. How many games did the Renegades win?

   A 72 games

   B 96 games

   C 108 games

   D 450 games

3. Rosa has a bag that contains 14 beads. The bag is 20% full. How many beads are in a full bag?

4. A music store ordered 400 CDs to hand out as prizes. They handed out 85% of these CDs. How many CDs did the store hand out?

5. The regular price of a baseball mitt is $75. It is on sale for 25% off. What is the sale price of the baseball mitt?

6. Mr. Nakai wants to leave a 15% tip on a meal that cost $42.

   a. How much should Mr. Nakai leave for a tip?

   b. What is the total that he paid for the meal including the tip?

7. During a 30% off sale, Chan Hee pays $175 for a picnic table. What was the original price of the picnic table?

   A $52.50
   B $227.50
   C $250.00
   D $483.33

8. The Gilroy Garlics won 40% of their 160 games. How many games did they win?

   A 64 games
   B 96 games
   C 108 games
   D 400 games

9. Yuet is in a gymnastics class that has 4 people. The class is 25% full. How many people are in a full gymnastics class?

10. What is 21 games out of every 100 games expressed as a percent?

11. The regular price of a softball mitt is $92. It is on sale for 35% off. What is the sale price of the softball mitt?

12. Mrs. Samuels wants to leave a 20% tip on a meal that cost $68.

    a. How much should Mrs. Samuels leave for a tip?

    b. What is the total that she paid for the meal including the tip?

Name _____

Common Core Standards Practice

6.RP.A.3d Use ratio and rate reasoning to solve real-world and mathematical problems, e.g., by reasoning about tables of equivalent ratios, tape diagrams, double number line diagrams, or equations. Use ratio reasoning to convert measurement units; manipulate and transform units appropriately when multiplying or dividing quantities.

1. Ayame drank 20 ounces of water in the morning, 36 ounces with lunch, and 20 ounces with dinner. How many cups of water did she drink?

   A 76

   B 9.5

   C 7.6

   D 4.75

2. A Girl Scout troop is placing markers every 16 meters along a trail. How many kilometers apart are the markers?

   A 0.016

   B 0.16

   C 1.6

   D 16

3. The length of a tennis court is 78 feet. How many inches long is the tennis court? Use equivalent ratios to find the solution.

4. A soup recipe calls for 4 pints of chicken stock. Your measuring cup holds only one cup. How many cups of chicken stock do you need? Use equivalent ratios to find the solution.

5. A chef made 4 liters of beef broth. She stored the broth in containers that hold 250 milliliters each. How many containers did she need? Use equivalent ratios to find the solution.

6. In 2010, the length of the Tour de France race course was 3,642 kilometers.

   a. How many meters long was the race?

   b. One mile is about 1.6 kilometers. About how many miles long was the course? Use equivalent ratios to find the solution.

CC 11

7. A sewing club is making quilts. Each quilt is 188 centimeters long. How many meters long is each quilt?

    A 0.0188 m

    B 0.188 m

    C 1.88 m

    D 18.8 m

8. Sue Jung is training for a race. When training she drinks a lot of water. On average, she drinks $9\frac{1}{2}$ cups of water. How many ounces of water does she drink?

    A 152 oz

    B 76 oz

    C 9.5 oz

    D 4.75 oz

9. Mr. Williams wants 16,000 pounds of stone for his driveway. However, the supply company only accepts orders in tons. How many tons of stone should Mr. Williams order? Use equivalent ratios to find the solution.

10. The length of a basketball court is 1,008 inches. How many feet long is a basketball court? Use equivalent ratios to find the solution.

11. You are making a punch recipe that calls for 4 quarts of juice. How many cups of juice do you need? Use equivalent ratios to find the solution.

12. An Ironman Triathlon is made up of three different segments, as shown in the table.

    a. How many meters long is each segment of the race?

Segment	Length
Swim	3.8 km
Bike	179.2 km
Run	42 km

    b. If 1 mile is about 1.6 kilometers, about how many miles long was each segment of the race?

Name _____

Common Core Standards Practice

6.NS.A.1 Interpret and compute quotients of fractions, and solve word problems involving division of fractions by fractions, e.g., by using visual fraction models and equations to represent the problem.

1. Marco has $1\frac{3}{4}$ pounds of potato salad. How many $\frac{1}{8}$-pound servings of potato salad can he make?

   A 12

   B 14

   C 16

   D 24

2. Which shows the quotient of the division equation shown?

   $$\frac{5}{12} \div \frac{1}{4} = \square$$

   A $1\frac{2}{3}$

   B $1\frac{1}{2}$

   C $\frac{3}{5}$

   D $\frac{5}{48}$

3. Use a model to divide 8 by $\frac{2}{3}$. Find the quotient.

4. Tonya's hummingbird feeder holds $\frac{1}{2}$ cup of liquid. Tonya fills the bird feeder with a spoon that holds $\frac{1}{8}$ cup. How many spoonfuls of liquid will fill the feeder?

   a. Write an equation that can be used to solve the problem.

   b. Solve the equation you wrote.

5. Find the quotient. $\frac{3}{4} \div \frac{4}{3}$.

6. Find the quotient. $\frac{5}{11} \div \frac{1}{8}$.

7. Mr. Santos has $\frac{3}{4}$ gallon of paint. He thinks he has enough paint to paint 4 chairs. How much paint should he plan to use on each chair? Draw a model to match the problem, and then solve.

8. The local animal shelter uses $1\frac{3}{5}$ bags of dog food each day to feed all of its dogs. For how many days will a donation of 12 bags of dog food last?

  a. Write an equation that can be used to determine for how many days the donated dog food will last.

  b. Solve the equation you wrote.

CC 14

Name _____

Common Core Standards Practice

6.NS.B.2 Fluently divide multi-digit numbers using the standard algorithm.

1. Which makes the equation true?

$$1{,}120 \div 32 = \boxed{}$$

A 25

B 32

C 35

D 36

2. Which makes the equation true?

$$540 \div 15 = \boxed{}$$

A 35 R10

B 36

C 36 R10

D 42

3. Find the quotient.

$$306 \div 18 = \boxed{}$$

4. Find the quotient.

$$725 \div 29 = \boxed{}$$

5. Find the quotient.

$$11{,}906 \div 312 = \boxed{}$$

6. Find the quotient.

$$5{,}134 \div 27 = \boxed{}$$

7. A cyclist traveled 2,448 miles in 36 days. What was the average number of miles the cyclist traveled per day?

8. Which makes the equation true?

$2{,}250 \div 125 = \boxed{}$

A 18 R10
B 18
C 17 R 100
D 17

9. Which makes the equation true?

$7{,}128 \div 216 = \boxed{}$

A 33
B 32 R116
C 43
D 38

10. Solve

$5{,}472 \div 152 = \boxed{}$

11. Divide 9,408 by 112.

12. Find the quotient.

$9{,}298 \div 84 = \boxed{}$

13. Find the quotient.

$6{,}716 \div 46 = \boxed{}$

14. Jon's Clothing Store made a total of 152 sales over the weekend. The sales totaled $5,472. What was the average amount per sale?

Common Core Standards Practice

6.NS.B.3 Fluently add, subtract, multiply, and divide multi-digit decimals using the standard algorithm for each operation.

1. Add $2.7 + 4.25 + 3.15$.

   A 5.85

   B 6.95

   C 7.4

   D 10.1

2. Find the quotient.

   $2.66 \div 3.5 = \boxed{}$

   A 0.32

   B 0.76

   C 0.87

   D 2.21

3. Find the difference.

   $289.37 - 283.49 = \boxed{}$

4. Multiply 22.65×3.82.

5. Find the quotient.

   $0.34\overline{)2.04}$

6. What is the product of 4.16 and 5.78?

7. Find the sum of 15.26, 9.58, and 16.78.

    A 24.84

    B 32.04

    C 41.62

    D 127.84

8. Find the quotient.

$$185.25 \div 3.25 = \boxed{}$$

    A 48

    B 57

    C 182

    D 602

9. Find the difference of $259.63 and $154.21.

10. Multiply.

$$\begin{array}{r} 63.4 \\ \times\ 9.15 \\ \hline \end{array}$$

11. Find the quotient.

$$6.1{\overline{\smash{\big)}\,75.03}}$$

12. The San Benedetto tunnel in Italy is 4.44 km long. The Cave Ovest Tunnel in Italy is 3.79 km long.

    a. Write an equation that can be used to determine the difference in length between the tunnels.

    b. Solve the equation you wrote.

Name _____

Common Core Standards Practice

6.NS.B.4 Find the greatest common factor of two whole numbers less than or equal to 100 and the least common multiple of two whole numbers less than or equal to 12. Use the distributive property to express a sum of two whole numbers 1–100 with a common factor as a multiple of a sum of two whole numbers with no common factor.

1. What is the greatest common factor of the numbers 12 and 54?

   A 2
   B 4
   C 6
   D 8

2. What is the greatest common factor of 16 and 72?

   A 4
   B 6
   C 8
   D 16

3. What is the greatest common factor of 80 and 95?

4. Find the greatest common factor of 48 and 57.

5. Rachel is making bouquets. She has 72 carnations and 48 roses. Each bouquet has the same number of flowers, with no flowers left over. What is the greatest number of bouquets she can make?

6. Adam volunteers once a month to make meals for shut-ins. He has 14 pieces of chicken and 21 pieces of corn. He needs to put the same number of pieces of chicken and corn on each plate.

   a. What is the greatest number of plates he can make?

   b. How many pieces of chicken and corn will he put on each plate?

7. What is the least common multiple of 8 and 6?

   A 24
   B 36
   C 48
   D 52

8. Which expression is equivalent to 24 + 15?

   A 2 × (12 + 7)
   B 3 × (8 + 5)
   C 5 × (8 + 3)
   D 8 × (3 + 7)

9. What is the least common multiple of 6 and 9?

10. What is the least common multiple of 12 and 8?

11. Myra can set up the chairs at tables with 8 or 10 per table with no chairs left over. What is the fewest number of chairs she could be setting up?

12. Which expressions are equivalent to 63 + 84? Circle all that are equivalent.

   9 × (7 + 9)   21 × (3 + 4)   3 × (21 + 84)

   7 × (9 + 12)   14 × (7 + 6)   3 × (21 + 28)

13. Write an expression for the area of this rectangle. Evaluate your expression to find the area.

14. Write at least two expressions equivalent to 36 + 24.

Name _____

Common Core Standards Practice

6.NS.C.5 Understand that positive and negative numbers are used together to describe quantities having opposite directions or values (e.g., temperature above/below zero, elevation above/below sea level, credits/debits, positive/negative electric charge); use positive and negative numbers to represent quantities in real-world contexts, explaining the meaning of 0 in each situation.

1. Which of the following represents a negative number? Circle all that apply.

   A deposit of $75

   B an increase of 2 inches in height

   C a debt of $2

   D a loss of 5 pounds in weight

2. Temperature can be measured in degrees Fahrenheit (°F). Which of these temperatures is the coldest?

   A 10°F

   B 0°F

   C 5°F

   D −10°F

3. Write an integer to represent 25 feet underground. Explain your answer.

4. Write an integer to represent a rise of 150 feet. Explain your answer.

5. During a football game, Howard's team gained 14 yards in one play and lost 12 yards in the next play. Write integers to represent the two plays.

6. Which of the following can be represented with −8? Circle all that apply.

   A A loss of $8

   B A rise of 8 feet up to sea level

   C A temperature 8 degrees below zero

   D An oil drill digging 8 miles below the surface

   E A deposit of $8 in a bank account

   F A change in temperature from 56°F to 64°F

7. Last week, Cy earned slightly more money than he spent. Is his net income represented by a positive number or a negative number? Explain.

8. A submarine travels 875 feet below sea level. Should the depth be represented by a positive number or a negative number? Explain.

9. During the day, the temperature changes from −5°F to +5°F.

   a. Does the temperature become warmer or cooler?

   b. Was the temperature that day ever 0°F? Explain how you know.

Name _____

Common Core Standards Practice

6.NS.C.6a Understand a rational number as a point on the number line. Extend number line diagrams and coordinate axes familiar from previous grades to represent points on the line and in the plane with negative number coordinates. Recognize opposite signs of numbers as indicating locations on opposite sides of 0 on the number line; recognize that the opposite of the opposite of a number is the number itself, e.g., $-(-3) = 3$, and that 0 is its own opposite.

1. What is the opposite of $-\frac{1}{2}$?

   A -2

   B $-\frac{1}{2}$

   C $\frac{1}{2}$

   D 2

2. Which of the following are the opposite of -5? Circle all that apply.

   A $-(-5)$

   B $-\frac{1}{5}$

   C $\frac{1}{5}$

   D 5

3. What is the opposite of 39?

4. Does $-(-0.7)$ equal -0.7 or $+0.7$?

5. Place 4 and -4 on the number line.

6. **a.** Name two integers that are opposites.

   b. How far from 0 is each integer on a number line?

7. What is the opposite of $\frac{4}{3}$?

8. Does the number $-(-98)$ equal -98 or $+98$?

9. What is the opposite of gaining 15 yards on a football play?

10. What is the opposite of -3.4?

11. Place 7 and its opposite on the number line.

12. The Coulomb (C) is a unit of electric charge. Two balloons together have a total electric charge of 0 C. What could be the charges on the individual balloons? Explain your answer.

Name _____

Common Core Standards Practice

6.NS.C.6b Understand a rational number as a point on the number line. Extend number line diagrams and coordinate axes familiar from previous grades to represent points on the line and in the plane with negative number coordinates. Understand signs of numbers in ordered pairs as indicating locations in quadrants of the coordinate plane; recognize that when two ordered pairs differ only by signs, the locations of the points are related by reflections across one or both axes.

1. In which quadrant is the point (−2, 3) located?

2. In which quadrant is the point (5, 8) located?

3. In which quadrant is the point (5, −8) located?

4. In which quadrant is the point (−2, −9) located?

5. Match the points to their coordinates.

    a. (−2, 4) _____

    b. (−2, −4) _____

    c. (−3, 1) _____

    d. (3, 1) _____

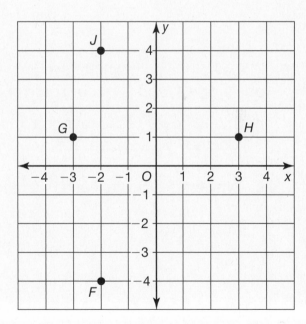

6. How do the points (6, 9) and (−6, 9) relate to each other? Explain your answer.

7. How do the points (−3, 5) and (−3, −5) relate to each other? Explain your answer.

8. How do the points (−4, 7) and (4, −7) relate to each other? Explain your answer.

9. Plot all of the points that have an x-coordinate of −1 or +1, and a y-coordinate of −3 or +3.

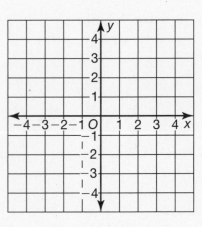

a. In how many of the four quadrants are the points located? _____

b. Why are the points each in a different quadrant?

Name _____

Common Core Standards Practice

6.NS.C.6c Understand a rational number as a point on the number line. Extend number line diagrams and coordinate axes familiar from previous grades to represent points on the line and in the plane with negative number coordinates. Find and position integers and other rational numbers on a horizontal or vertical number line diagram; find and position pairs of integers and other rational numbers on a coordinate plane.

1. Name the integer represented by the points.

    a. N _____

    b. P _____

    c. Q _____

    d. S _____

2. Name the integer represented by the points.

    a. F _____

    b. G _____

    c. H _____

    d. J _____

CC 27

3. Write the coordinates of each point.

    a. *M* _____

    b. *K* _____

    c. *H* _____

    d. *O* _____

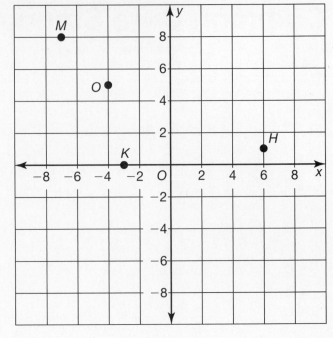

4. Plot and label each point on the coordinate grid.

    a. point *A* at (−4, 8)

    b. point *B* at (5, −2)

    c. point *C* at (−7, 0)

    d. point *D* at (3, −10)

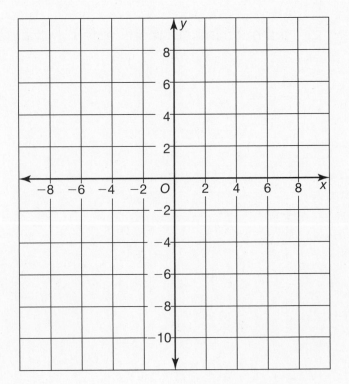

CC 28

Name _____

Common Core Standards Practice

6.NS.C.7a Understand ordering and absolute value of rational numbers. Interpret statements of inequality as statements about the relative position of two numbers on a number line diagram.

1. The statement $-8 < -2$ compares the numbers -8 and -2.

   a. Plot -8 and -2 on the number line shown below.

   b. How does the statement $-8 < -2$ explain the positions of the numbers on a horizontal number line?

2. **a.** Plot the numbers $|5|$ and -3 on the number line shown below.

   b. Write a statement to compare the positions of $|5|$ and -3 on the number line.

3. **a.** Plot the numbers -4 and -7 on the number line shown below.

   b. Write an inequality to compare the two numbers.

   c. How does the statement you wrote explain the position of the two numbers on the number line?

4. How does the statement $-38 > -77$ explain the positions of the numbers on a horizontal number line?

5. a. Plot the numbers -40 and 25 on the number line shown below.

b. Write an inequality to compare the two numbers.

c. How are the positions of the two numbers on the number line explained by the statement you wrote?

6. a. Plot the numbers -60 and -70 on the number line shown below.

b. Write an inequality to compare the two numbers.

c. How does the statement you wrote explain the position of the two numbers on the number line?

Name _____

Common Core Standards Practice

6.NS.C.7b Understand ordering and absolute value of rational numbers. Write, interpret, and explain statements of order for rational numbers in real-world contexts.

1. One bag of tomatoes weighs $5\frac{3}{4}$ pounds. A second bag weighs $5\frac{3}{8}$ pounds. Write an inequality to compare the weights of the two bags.

2. At the stock market, the price of Best Tea dropped $3.25 per share while the price of Yummy Tea dropped $3.33. Which company had the smaller price drop? Explain.

3. Julio and Reggie each filled a 1-liter bottle with a sports drink before their soccer game. At half time, Julio has 0.66 liter of sports drink left in his bottle and Reggie has 0.6 liter in his bottle.

   a. Who has more sports drink in his bottle? Write a number statement to explain your answer.

   b. Who drank more of his sports drink in the first half of the game? Write a number statement to explain your answer.

4. Four students ran the 100-meter dash. Their times are shown in the table.

Runner	Horatio	Uma	Aidan	Fiona
Time (seconds)	14.32	16.25	13.75	14.56

   a. Write the times of the students from least to greatest.

   b. Which student won the race? Explain.

5. The menu prices of a lasagna dish at several restaurants are shown below.

Restaurant	Italia	Fabio's	Maria's	Roma
Cost of Lasagna	$12.95	$12.25	$11.50	$12.99

a. Order the costs of the dishes from greatest to least.

b. Which restaurant has the most expensive dish? Which has the least expensive?

6. At 6 A.M. the temperature was −3.2°C. At 11 A.M. the temperature was −2.1°C. At 3 P.M. the temperature was −3.7°C. Write the temperatures from least to greatest.

7. The table below shows the distances in miles that 4 students live from the library.

Student	Yvonne	Stevie	Jose	Chiara
Miles from Library	$\frac{12}{5}$	$3\frac{1}{2}$	$\frac{12}{10}$	0.75

a. List the students in order from closest to farthest away from the library. Show your work.

b. Can you tell which student lives closest to Stevie? Explain.

Name _____

Common Core Standards Practice

6.NS.C.7c Understand ordering and absolute value of rational numbers. Understand the absolute value of a rational number as its distance from 0 on the number line; interpret absolute value as magnitude for a positive or negative quantity in a real-world situation.

1. Which of these has an absolute value of 5? Circle all that apply.

-10	-5	-0.5
15	0.05	5

2. What of these has an absolute value of 2.5? Circle all that apply.

5	-2.5	0.25
2.5	-0.25	1.25

3. Which numbers have a distance of 6 units from 0? Circle all that apply.

$-12,$	-6	$-3,$	-0.6
$0.6,$	$3,$	6	12

4. Which two numbers are each a distance of 8 units from 0?

A -8 and 0

B -8 and 8

C -16 and 16

D -16 and 0

5. What positive number has an absolute value of $\frac{2}{9}$?

6. What negative number has an absolute value of 4.25?

7. A man dives 21 feet into the ocean from sea level. Write an expression to represent the vertical distance he travels.

8. Which of these numbers has an absolute value of 3? Circle all that apply.

-3　　　　6　　　　$-\frac{6}{2}$

$\frac{2}{6}$　　　　3　　　　0.3

9. Which of these numbers have an absolute value of 8?

16　　　　-8　　　　$\frac{16}{2}$

8　　　　$\frac{4}{2}$　　　　-16

10. List at least three numbers that have an absolute value of $\frac{1}{2}$.

11. What is the value of $-\left|-3\frac{1}{2}\right|$?

12. Explain why both -4 and 4 have the same absolute value.

13. List at least 3 rational numbers that have an absolute value of 2.

14. A bird flew 12 meters down from a tree branch to the ground. Write an expression to represent the vertical distance the bird flew from the tree to the ground.

CC 34

Name _____

Common Core Standards Practice

6.NS.C.7d Understand ordering and absolute value of rational numbers. Distinguish comparisons of absolute value from statements about order.

1. Maria withdrew $45 and $65 from her savings account.

   a. Write two integers to represent the changes to the savings account.

   b. Which integer is greater?

   c. Which withdrawal changed the account more? Explain.

2. The temperature on Monday was 6°C below zero. On Tuesday, the temperature was 11°C below zero.

   a. Write two integers to represent the temperatures.

   b. Which temperature is higher?

   c. Between Monday and Tuesday, did the temperature increase or decrease? Explain.

3. Jacques and Fatima start the day at the beach, which is at sea level. Then Jacques climbs a hill that is 24 feet above sea level, while Fatima dives into the ocean to a depth of 30 feet below sea level.

   a. Write two integers to represent the distances in this situation.

   b. Which integer is greater? Explain.

   c. Who had the greater vertical change in distance to sea level? Explain.

4. Ms. Frank owes her bank $94, and she owes a neighbor $87.

  a. Which number is greater, −94 or −87?

  b. Does Ms. Frank owe more money to the bank or the neighbor? To explain your answer, write a number statement that uses absolute value.

5. In one play of a football game, the home team lost 17 yards. In the next play, the home team gained 4 yards.

  a. Write two integers to represent the amounts in the situation.

  b. Which number is greater?

  c. In which play did the team's position on the field change the most? Explain your answer with a number statement that includes absolute value.

6. Louis and Fran are fishing on a deep lake. Louis lowers his lure to a depth of 120 feet. Fran lowers her lure to a depth of 25 feet.

  a. Write two integers to represent the depths of the lures.

  b. Which number is greater?

  c. Whose lure is farther from the boat? Explain your answer with a number sentence that includes absolute value.

Name _____

Common Core Standards Practice

6.NS.C.8 Solve real-world and mathematical problems by graphing points in all four quadrants of the coordinate plane. Include use of coordinates and absolute value to find distances between points with the same first coordinate or the same second coordinate.

1. a. Graph and label these points in the coordinate plane.

A: (0, 2) B: (−1, −3)

C: (−2, −4) D: (1, −1)

E: (−1, 4)

b. What is the distance between points B and E?

c. Explain how to use absolute value to find the distance between points B and E.

2. Judi lives at (−1, −4). To get to the library, she walks 3 blocks to the right and then 2 blocks up the coordinate grid.

a. Graph the point where Judy lives. Label the point A.

b. Graph the point that shows Judy's position after she walks 3 blocks to the right. Label the point B.

c. Graph the point where the library is. Label the point C.

d. How many blocks did Judy walk?

CC 37

3. a. Graph (−1, −2) and (2, −2) on the coordinate plane.

b. What is the distance between the two points?

c. Tell how you found the distance between the points.

4. a. Graph and label the points in the coordinate plane. Then draw lines to connect the points into a trapezoid.

A: (−5, −3) B: (2, −3)

C: (1, 2) D: (−4, 2)

b. Find the distance between points C and D and the distance between points A and B.

5. What is the distance between (−2, 3) and (−2, −5) on the coordinate plane? Explain how you determined the distance.

CC 38

Name _____

Common Core Standards Practice

6.EE.A.1 Write and evaluate numerical expressions involving whole-number exponents.

1. Which is the value of 3^3?

    A 6

    B 9

    C 27

    D 81

2. Which is an equivalent expression for

$0.14 \cdot 0.14 \cdot 0.14 \cdot 0.14 \cdot 0.14$?

    A $(0.14)^5$

    B $5(0.14)$

    C $0.14 + 5$

    D $(0.14)^{\frac{1}{5}}$

3. Evaluate the expression below.

5^4

4. Write the expression below with a single exponent.

$\frac{1}{3} \cdot \frac{1}{3} \cdot \frac{1}{3} \cdot \frac{1}{3}$

5. Which of these expressions is equivalent to 129?

    A $9^2 + 3 \cdot 4^2$

    B $7^2 \cdot 3 - 4 \cdot 7$

    C $3(2^3 \cdot 5 + 3)$

    D $5^3 + 2^2$

    E $6 \cdot 3^3 - 5 \cdot 7$

    F $2^7 + 2^0$

6. Which is the value of $\left(\frac{1}{7}\right)^2$?

    A 14

    B $\frac{1}{14}$

    C $\frac{1}{27}$

    D $\frac{1}{49}$

7. Which is the value of $(0.1)^3$?

   A 0.0001

   B 0.001

   C 0.3

   D 3.1

8. Which is an equivalent expression for (5.1)(5.1)? Circle all that apply.

   A 5.1 + 5.1

   B 5.1 × 2

   C 2(5.1) × 5.1

   D 5.1^2

   E 25 + 0.1

   F $5^2 + 2 \cdot 5 \cdot 0.1 + 0.1^2$

9. Write a mathematical expression for the phrase below.

Three more than twice the square of six

10. Write an expression with an exponent that is equivalent to the expression below.

$$\frac{1}{6} \times \frac{1}{6} \times \frac{1}{6} \times \frac{1}{6}$$

11. Simplify.

$$4^3 - 6 \cdot 3^2$$

12. Simplify.

$$3^3 - 3^2$$

Name _____

Common Core Standards Practice

6.EE.A.2a Write, read, and evaluate expressions in which letters stand for numbers. Write expressions that record operations with numbers and with letters standing for numbers.

1. Which expression represents this phrase?

   three times the sum of the number y and nine

   A $y + 9$
   B $3y + 9$
   C $y + 3(9)$
   D $3(y + 9)$

2. Which expression represents this phrase?

   five times of the sum of nineteen and a number k

   A $5(19k)$
   B $5(19) + k$
   C $5 + 19k$
   D $5(19 + k)$

3. Which expression represents this phrase?

   eight more than four times the number z

   A $z + 8$
   B $4z + 8$
   C $z + 4 \cdot 8$
   D $4(z + 8)$

4. Which expression represents this phrase?

   two-thirds of the sum of four and a number p

   A $\frac{2}{3}(4p)$

   B $\frac{2}{3}(4 + p)$

   C $\frac{2}{3}(4 - p)$

   D $\frac{2}{3}p$

5. Write an expression to represent this phrase.

   Five more than six times the difference of a number and eight

6. Write an expression to represent this phrase.

   the product of twelve and six less than the number q

7. Write expressions for these phrases.

   a. a number *c* divided by two

   b. the number *r* less than 14

   c. the sum of a number *x* and 2 divided by 3

   d. four divided by two more than the number *x*

   e. the number *x* divided by two more than the number *x*

8. Write a mathematical expression for each phrase.

   a. the quotient of 11 and a number *s*

   b. six times a number *x*

   c. a number *w* minus 7

   d. three times the sum of a number *w* and 7

   e. six times the sum of a number *x* and four

Name _____

Common Core Standards Practice

6.EE.A.2b Write, read, and evaluate expressions in which letters stand for numbers. Identify parts of an expression using mathematical terms (sum, term, product, factor, quotient, coefficient); view one or more parts of an expression as a single entity.

1. How many terms are in this expression?

   $4x + 3y - 12x + 5$

   A 2
   B 3
   C 4
   D 5

2. Which statement best describes this expression?

   $3x - 5y + 6x + 8 + 10y$

   A The expression is the sum of 5 terms.
   B The expression is the product of 5 terms and 2 variables.
   C The factors of the expression are 3, 5, 6, 8, and 10.
   D The expression is the sum of the factors 3, 5, 6, 8, and 10.

3. What are the coefficients of this expression?

   $10x + x - 7y + 8y$

4. What is the coefficient of the r-term in this expression?

   $-8r + 24s - 9r - 7$

5. How many terms are in this expression?

   $2x - 11x + 7$

   A 2
   B 3
   C 4
   D 5

6. List the terms of this expression.

   $-9x - 5x - 7p - 3p$

7. $2w(w + 9)$

  a. How many factors are in this expression?

  b. What are the factors?

8. Describe the parts of this expression. Use mathematical terms, such as *product, factor,* and *quotient.*

$\frac{x}{8} + 3y$

What is $\frac{x}{8}$? _____

What is $3y$? _____

9. Describe the parts of this expression. Use mathematical terms, such as *product, factor,* and *quotient.*

$\frac{5 - x}{3} - \frac{y}{7}$

What is $\frac{5 - x}{3}$? _____

What is $\frac{y}{7}$? _____

10. List two factors of $2(x + 7)$.

CC 44

Name _____

Common Core Standards Practice

6.EE.A.2c Write, read, and evaluate expressions in which letters stand for numbers. Evaluate expressions at specific values of their variables. Include expressions that arise from formulas used in real-world problems. Perform arithmetic operations, including those involving whole-number exponents, in the conventional order when there are no parentheses to specify a particular order (Order of Operations).

1. Evaluate the expression for $x = 10$ and $y = 3$.

   $5(x - 2y)$

   A 10

   B 20

   C 40

   D 50

2. Evaluate the expression $d + 15p$ for $d = 75$ and $p = 60$.

3. The area of a square is given by the formula $A = s^2$. What is the area of a square with a side length s of 6 in.?

4. Evaluate the expression for $m = \frac{1}{4}$ and $p = -3$.

   $\dfrac{6m}{p}$

5. Consider the expression below.

   $K = t + \dfrac{s}{3}$

   If $t = 5$ and $s = 9$, what is the value of K?

6. The formula $d = 15t$ describes the distance d in miles that Peter can ride his bike in t hours. How far does he ride in 3 hours?

7. The area of a triangle is given by the formula $A = \frac{1}{2}bh$ in which b is the base of the triangle and h is the height of the triangle. What is the area of a triangle with a base of 2.5 m and a height of 1.2 m?

A 1.5 m²

B 1.85 m²

C 3 m²

D 3.7 m²

8. The perimeter P of a rectangle can be calculated with the formula $P = 2l + 2w$, in which l is the length and w is the width. What is the perimeter of a rectangle with a length of 8 cm and a width of 2.3 cm?

A 16 cm

B 18.4 cm

C 20.6 cm

D 23.69 cm

9. The volume of a rectangular prism is given by the formula $V = l \times w \times h$. What is the volume of a rectangular prism with a length of 10 cm, a width of $6\frac{1}{2}$ cm, and a height of $2\frac{1}{4}$ cm?

10. Consider the expression below.

$2t + 4w$

Evaluate the expression for $t = 3$ and $w = 0.2$.

11. Consider the expression below.

$$\frac{3x + 2y}{4}$$

Evaluate the expression for $x = 2$ and $y = 0.5$.

12. Evaluate the expression for $f = 5$ and $g = 11$.

$3f + 2g - 16$

Common Core Standards Practice

6.EE.A.3 Apply the properties of operations to generate equivalent expressions.

1. Which expression is equivalent to $3(x + 5)$?

   A $3x + 5$

   B $3x + 15$

   C $x + 15$

   D $x + 8$

2. Which expression is equivalent to $2(3v + 7)$?

   A $6v - 7$

   B $3v + 14$

   C $6v + 14$

   D $6v + 7$

3. Which property can be used to show that $4r + 3s + 2r = 6r + 3s$? Explain your answer.

4. Explain why $2(3t - w)$ is equivalent to $6t - 2w$.

5. How are these two sets of equivalent expressions similar?

   $$24 + 84 = 12(2 + 7) \qquad\qquad 5 + 10x = 5(1 + 2x)$$

6. **a.** Write an expression equivalent to $3w - 3w + 3w$ with just one term.

   b. What property or properties applies?

7. Jorge says that $4(x + 3) + 5$ is equal to $4x - 17$. Is he right? Explain your answer.

8. Which expression is equivalent to $3y + 3y + 3y + 3y$?

   A $12y$

   B $81y$

   C $3y^4$

   D $6y$

9. Which expression is equivalent to $15m + 18$?

   A $15m - 18$

   B $5m + 18$

   C $5m + 6$

   D $3(5m + 6)$

10. Use the distributive property to write an expression equivalent to $7(9x - 5)$.

11. How are these two sets of equivalent expressions similar?

   $76 + 102 + 24 = (76 + 24) + 102$ $2x + 3y - 12 + x = (2x + x) + 3y - 12$

12. Markie wrote these expressions on the board.

   $8(0.3x + 2.6) = 2.4x + 20.8$

   Is Markie's work correct? Explain your answer.

13. Explain why $x + y + x + y$ is equivalent to $2x + 2y$.

14. Which property can be used to show that $4r + 12s + 20t = 4(r + 3s + 5t)$? Explain your answer.

Name _____

Common Core Standards Practice

6.EE.A.4 Identify when two expressions are equivalent (i.e., when the two expressions name the same number regardless of which value is substituted into them).

1. Which expression is equivalent to $5s + 4$?

    A $4(s + 1)$

    B $9s$

    C $5(s + 1)$

    D $s + s + s + s + s + 4$

2. Which expression is equivalent to the expression below?

    $42r - 42$

    A $7(r - 6)$

    B $6(r - 7)$

    C $41r$

    D $42(r - 1)$

3. Simplify $x - 3x + (9 - 2) + 5x$.

4. Simplify $y + 7y - (3y + 7)$.

5. Which of these expressions is equivalent to $3g + 21$? Circle all that apply.

    $3(g + 7)$ $3(g - 7)$ $3(g + 21)$ $3(g - 21)$

6. Which of these expressions is equivalent to $w + w - w + 6$? Circle all that apply.

    $3w + 6$ $w + 6$ $3 + 3 - (3 - w)$ $w - 6$

7. Find the expression that is equivalent to the expression below.

$3(2d - 5)$

A $-15 - 6d$

B $15 - 2d$

C $6d + 15$

D $6d - 15$

8. Find the expression that is equivalent to the expression below.

$6y + (2y - 3) + 6$

A $12y - 3$

B $8y - 9$

C $4y + 3$

D $8y + 3$

9. Simplify the expression.

$(5 + 2x) + (2x + 6) + 1$

10. Simplify the expression.

$4g + 5 - g - g + 2 + g$

11. Write the expression $6x - 8$ as the product of 2 and another factor.

12. Write the expression $15 - 5y$ as the product of 5 and another factor.

13. Write the expression $4x + 8$ as the product of 4 and another factor.

Name _____

Common Core Standards Practice

6.EE.B.5 Understand solving an equation or inequality as a process of answering a question: which values from a specified set, if any, make the equation or inequality true? Use substitution to determine whether a given number in a specified set makes an equation or inequality true. Which value of t makes the inequality true?

1. Which values of t make the inequality true? Circle all that apply.

   $4t - 1 < 12$

1	6	4

5	3	2

2. Which values of w make the inequality true? Circle all that apply.

   $5w - 1 > 17$

8	6	4

5	3	2

3. Which values of t make the inequality true? Circle all that apply.

   $t + 6 \leq 14$

10	5	8

15	12	7

4. Which values for m from the set $\{3, 5, 7\}$ make the inequality true?

   $5m - 6 < 20$

5. Which value from the set $\{2, 6, 8\}$ makes $3x - 5 = 13$ true?

6. Which values for m from the set $\{\frac{1}{2}, \frac{1}{10}, \frac{1}{5}\}$ make the inequality true?

   $2m \geq \frac{1}{10}$

7. Is 5 a solution to the inequality below? Explain how you know.

   $x - 3 > 2$

8. Is 12 a solution to the inequality below? Explain how you know.

   $24 - y \leq 12$

9. Which values for t make the inequality true?

$35 - 4t > 7$

8	6	4
7	10	9

10. Which value for x makes the equation true?

$x + \frac{1}{8} = \frac{3}{4}$

A $\frac{1}{2}$

B $\frac{5}{8}$

C $\frac{3}{4}$

D 1

11. Which values for x from the set $\{2, 4, 6\}$ make the inequality true?

$25 - 4x < 3$

12. Which value for a from the set $\{0, 5, 9\}$ makes the equation true?

$a + 5 = 14$

13. Which values for g from the set $\{0.4, 0.2, 0.6\}$ make the equation true?

$5g = 1$

14. Which values for y make the inequality true?

$0.2y > 1$

A 0.5

B 5

C 7

D 10

15. Is 7 a solution to the equation below? Explain how you know.

$2y + 3 = 20$

16. Is 8 a solution to the inequality below? Explain how you know.

$3x - (4 + x) \geq 12$

Name _____

Common Core Standards Practice

6.EE.B.6 Use variables to represent numbers and write expressions when solving a real-world or mathematical problem; understand that a variable can represent an unknown number, or, depending on the purpose at hand, any number in a specified set.

1. Chi has five fewer than twice as many markers as Rosa. Rosa has x markers. Which expression represents the number of markers that Chi has?

A $(5 + 2)x$

B $2x - 5$

C $2x + 5$

D $x + 5 - 2$

2. Juanita earns money by mowing lawns. She charges each customer $8 for expenses plus $12 per hour. Which expression can be used to determine how much Juanita earns mowing a lawn for h hours?

A $12h + 8$

B $12h - 8$

C $8h + 12$

D $8h - 12$

3. At a school carnival, Jasmine paid $5 for admission and $1.25 per ride. Write an algebraic expression to represent the total amount Jasmine spent in dollars if she went on t rides.

4. Mato had 18 video games. He won g video games in a contest. Write an algebraic expression for the number of video games that Mato has now.

5. Marita has $100 to buy new clothes. She wants to buy a pair of jeans for $35 and some tops that each cost $27. Her older sister tells her she can use the equation $100 - 35 = 27t$ to determine how many tops she can buy.

a. What does t represent in the equation?

b. Is Marita's sister correct? Explain.

Match the expressions to the situation. Some expressions may not match any situation. Some may match more than one situation.

6. **a.** Kelsey has three more than five times the number of seashells Hahn has.

      $65h + 15$

  b. A county fair charges each attendee $15 for admission and $2.00 per ride ticket.

      $65 + h$

  c. An appliance repairman charges $65 per hour plus a service fee of $15.

      $15 + 2t$

  d. Emilio bought a skateboard and a helmet. He spent $65 on the skateboard and some money for the helmet.

      $5x + 3$

  e. Rana had $15 at the start of week. During the week, she bought two songs online.

      $3w - 5$

7. Mrs. Andrews sent Phil and Frank to the store with $20. They need to buy bread that costs $3.50, and a dozen eggs that cost $2. The two boys can spend the rest of the money on snacks that cost $1.50 each. Phil says they can use the equation $20 - (3.50 - 2) = 1.5s$ to determine how many snacks they can buy.

  a. What does s represent in the equation?

  b. Is Phil correct? Explain.

Common Core Standards Practice

6.EE.B.7 Solve real-world and mathematical problems by writing and solving equations of the form $x + p = q$ and $px = q$ for cases in which p, q and x are all nonnegative rational numbers.

1. Gabriela spent $83.97 on three jackets. Each jacket cost the same amount. Write an algebraic equation to show the cost of one jacket. Solve the equation.

2. Yomi has a job shoveling snow. She charges $18 for each driveway shoveled. One winter day she made $108. Write an equation to show the number of driveways she shoveled. Solve the equation.

3. Chan Hee is paid $25 for tutoring. Then he spends $4 on a sandwich and $2 on a drink. Write an equation to show the amount of money Chan Hee has now. Solve the equation.

4. A school spent $149.25 on baseballs. Each baseball cost $1.99. Write an equation to show the number of baseballs purchased by the school. Solve the equation.

5. Tell how to solve for w. Then solve.

   $w + 1\frac{1}{3} = 6$

6. Tell how to solve for h. Then solve.

   $h - \frac{3}{5} = \frac{7}{4}$

7. Tell how to solve for t. Then solve.

$t + 2.34 = 6.89$

8. Solve. $y - 1\frac{1}{4} = 8\frac{1}{2}$

9. Sophia spent $33.40 on four bracelets. Each bracelet cost the same amount. Write an equation to show the cost of one bracelet. Solve the equation.

10. Lakeisha has a babysitting job. She charges $7 per hour. One week she earned $168. Write an equation to show the number of hours Lakeisha babysat that week. Solve the equation.

11. Anton won $30 for running in a race. He spends $12 on a shirt and $6 on lunch. Write an equation to show the amount of money Anton has left. Solve the equation.

12. A summer recreation league has 72 girls signed up for softball. Each softball team has 12 players. Write an equation to show the number of teams that could be formed. Solve the equation.

Name _____

Common Core Standards Practice

6.EE.B.8 Write an inequality of the form $x > c$ or $x < c$ to represent a constraint or condition in a real-world or mathematical problem. Recognize that inequalities of the form $x > c$ or $x < c$ have infinitely many solutions; represent solutions of such inequalities on number line diagrams.

1. A table can seat at most 8 people. Represent the number of people who can sit at the table as an inequality.

2. A package of pasta states to cook the pasta for up to 11 minutes.

   a. Represent this as an inequality.

   b. What are some possible numbers of minutes the pasta can cook?

3. A roller coaster rider must be at least 54 inches tall.

   a. Represent the height of a roller coaster rider as an inequality.

   b. Graph the inequality on the number line.

4. Campers are told to bring at least 10 pairs of socks for a camping trip.

   a. Represent the numbers of pairs of socks as an inequality.

   b. What are some possible numbers of pairs of socks a camper would bring?

5. A cell phone plan offers up to 700 free minutes every month.

   a. Represent the number of free minutes as an inequality.

   b. Graph this inequality on a number line.

6. The altitude of a plane must always be no less than 200 feet above ground except during take off and landing.

    a. Represent the flying altitude of the plane as an inequality.

    b. Graph the inequality on the number line.

    c. How many solutions does this inequality have? Explain your answer.

7. Match the inequality to the situation. Some situations may not match to an inequality.

    a. DeShawn reads at least 3 books each month. $x > 35$

    b. A soccer team roster can have no more than 20 active players. $x \le 20$

    c. Angie puts at least 6 flowers in each flower arrangement. $x \ge 3$

    d. Riders of this ride must be over 35 inches tall. $x < 20$

    e. Maya can invite no more than 15 people to her party. $x \ge 6$

8. Classes at Jonas' school can not have more than 15 students.

Graph this inequality on a number line.

Name _____

Common Core Standards Practice

6.EE.C.9 Use variables to represent two quantities in a real-world problem that change in relationship to one another; write an equation to express one quantity, thought of as the dependent variable, in terms of the other quantity, thought of as the independent variable. Analyze the relationship between the dependent and independent variables using graphs and tables, and relate these to the equation.

1. What is the relationship between the two variables?

x	y
1	4.5
2	9
3	13.5
4	18

2. Complete the table.
$y = 3x - 2$

x	y
1	1
2	
	7
4	

3. Use the graph to describe the change in y as x increases by 1.

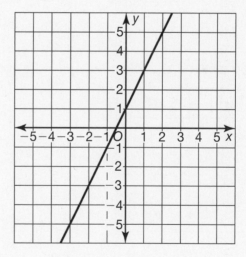

4. Write an equation that represents the relationship between the two variables.

x	1	2	3	4
y	9	16	23	30

5. The number of baseball cards in an album, c, depends on the number of pages, p. The equation $c = 9p$ is used to determine the number of cards. Complete the table.

p	c
1	
	18
8	

6. A cable company charges $25 per month and $5 for every pay-per-view movie ordered.

a. Write the equation that represents the situation. Let B represent the total bill and m represent the number of pay-per-view movies.

b. Complete the table.

m	B
1	30
2	
3	
	65

c. Graph the solution.

Name _____

Common Core Standards Practice

6.G.A.1 Find the area of right triangles, other triangles, special quadrilaterals, and polygons by composing into rectangles or decomposing into triangles and other shapes; apply these techniques in the context of solving real-world and mathematical problems.

1. Which is the area of a triangle with base length 6 units and height 9 units?

   A 3 square units

   B 15 square units

   C 27 square units

   D 54 square units

2. Find the area of the parallelogram.

   A 12 in.²

   B 24 in.²

   C 28 in.²

   D 32 in.²

3. a. Compose the right triangle into a rectangle.

   b. Explain how to use the composed rectangle to find the area of the triangle.

4. a. Decompose the trapezoid into rectangles and/or triangles.

   b. Find the areas of the shapes you used in part (a).

   c. Find the area of the trapezoid.

5. What is the area of the figure?

9 in.

6 in.

3 in.

4 in.

5 in.

6 in.

6. Fujita is making a pennant. How much material does he need to make the pennant?

7 ft

9 ft

7. A company is making a tile design. Each tile is an 8-in. by 8 in. square. How many triangular pieces shown below fit inside each square tile?

4 in.

2 in.

8. The floor of a work shed has the shape of a trapezoid as shown. What is the area of the floor?

8 ft

6 ft

4 ft

Name _____

Common Core Standards Practice

6.G.A.2 Find the volume of a right rectangular prism with fractional edge lengths by packing it with unit cubes of the appropriate unit fraction edge lengths, and show that the volume is the same as would be found by multiplying the edge lengths of the prism. Apply the formulas $V = lwh$ and $V = bh$ to find volumes of right rectangular prisms with fractional edge lengths in the context of solving real-world and mathematical problems.

1. A flower box has the shape of a rectangular prism and is 3 ft long, $2\frac{1}{2}$ ft wide, and $\frac{1}{2}$ ft deep. How many cubic feet of potting soil will it hold?

   A $1\frac{1}{2}$ ft³

   B $3\frac{3}{4}$ ft³

   C 6 ft³

   D $7\frac{1}{2}$ ft³

2. A rectangular prism has a length of $10\frac{1}{3}$ in., a width of 6 in., and a height of $9\frac{1}{4}$ in.

   a. Draw a diagram of the prism.

   b. Determine the volume of the rectangular prism.

3. Marcus is packing a large box with some small boxes. The large box has the shape of a rectangular prism and is $2\frac{1}{2}$ ft long, $1\frac{1}{2}$ ft wide, and 2 ft tall. Each small box is cube-shaped with a side length of $\frac{1}{2}$ ft. How many of the small boxes will fit in the large box?

4. A rectangular swimming pool is 25 ft long and $20\frac{1}{2}$ ft wide, and it must be filled to a depth of $4\frac{1}{2}$ ft. One cubic foot of water is equal to $7\frac{1}{2}$ gallons. How many gallons of water will it take to fill the pool?

5. Jaipal is making a small planter box. The box is $\frac{1}{2}$ foot long, $\frac{2}{3}$ foot wide, and $\frac{7}{8}$ foot deep. Jaipal has $\frac{1}{4}$ cubic foot of potting soil. Will the potting soil fit in the planter? Explain.

6. Which is the volume of the rectangular prism shown below?

$\frac{1}{2}$ yard

$\frac{1}{4}$ yard

$1\frac{3}{4}$ yards

A $\frac{3}{32}$ cubic yard

B $\frac{7}{32}$ cubic yard

C $2\frac{1}{2}$ cubic yards

D 5 cubic yards

7. A fish tank has the following dimensions: $24\frac{1}{2}$ in. long, $12\frac{1}{2}$ in. wide, and $12\frac{3}{4}$ in. tall. What is the volume of the fish tank?

Name _____

Common Core Standards Practice

6.G.A.3 Draw polygons in the coordinate plane given coordinates for the vertices; use coordinates to find the length of a side joining points with the same first coordinate or the same second coordinate. Apply these techniques in the context of solving real-world and mathematical problems.

1. A graphic designer is making letters for a varsity jacket. He is drawing the letters on a coordinate grid. One of the letters has the following vertices: (4, −1), (4, −3), (−2, −3), (−2, 5), (0, 5), (0, −1)

   Plot the points and connect them to form a polygon. What letter is formed?

2. a. What is the distance from point *A* to point *B*?

   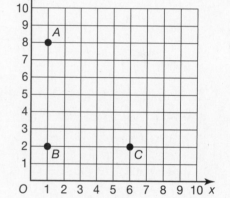

   b. What is the distance from point *B* to point *C*?

3. Mia draws a map of her city on a coordinate grid. The park is located at (−3, 2), the library is located at (1, 2), and Mia's home is located at (1, −1).

   a. Plot the locations on a coordinate grid. Each unit on the grid represents 1 mile.

   b. What shape is formed by joining the three points?

   c. What is the distance from the park to the library?

   d. What is the distance from the library to Mia's house?

CC 65

4. The following coordinates are the vertices of a polygon: (2, 1), (2, 7), (7, 7), and (7, 1).

    a. Plot the points and connect them to form a polygon.

    b. What is the perimeter of the polygon?

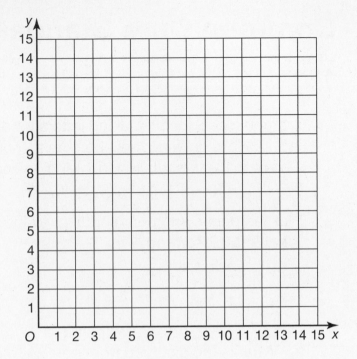

5. Rectangle *ABCD* has vertices $A(1\frac{1}{2}, 8)$, $B(6\frac{1}{2}, 8)$, $C(6\frac{1}{2}, 2\frac{1}{2})$, and $D(1\frac{1}{2}, 2\frac{1}{2})$.

    a. Plot the points on a coordinate grid.

    b. Which sides of the rectangle are longest? Explain how you know.

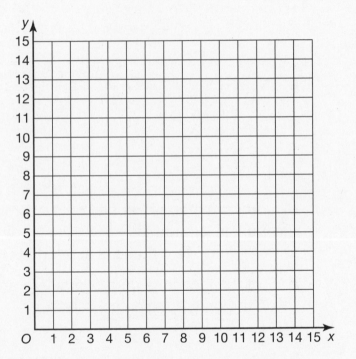

Name _____

Common Core Standards Practice

6.G.A.4 Represent three-dimensional figures using nets made up of rectangles and triangles, and use the nets to find the surface area of these figures. Apply these techniques in the context of solving real-world and mathematical problems.

1. Which net will form a cube?

A

B

C

D

2. Draw a net for a rectangular prism.

3. A cereal box in the shape of a rectangular prism has the dimensions shown below.

15 in.

3 in.

12 in.

a. Draw a net of the cereal box and label the dimensions.

b. Calculate the surface area of the cereal box.

4. Describe the shapes of the faces that are needed to construct a square pyramid and then draw a net of this figure.

5. Which figure will the given net form?

A

B

C

D

6. A movie theater is designing a new container for its popcorn. The new container has the shape of a rectangular pyramid as shown below.

12 in.

10 in. 8 in.

a. Draw a net of the new container.

b. Calculate the surface area of the container.

c. The company that makes the containers charges $.02 per square inch of container material. How much will 500 containers cost?

Name _____

Common Core Standards Practice

6.SP.A.1 Recognize a statistical question as one that anticipates variability in the data related to the question and accounts for it in the answers.

1. Which of these is a statistical question?

 A You ask a friend, "When is your birthday?"

 B You ask several people, "In what year were you born?"

 C You ask all of your friends, "What year is this?"

 D You ask a parent, "What time is it?"

2. Which of these is a NOT statistical question?

 A You ask a friend, "What movie do you want to see?"

 B You ask your friends, "Did you see the latest Transformers movie?"

 C You ask many of your classmates, "Which Harry Potter movie did you like best?"

 D You ask several people, "What did you think of the movie you just saw?"

3. Sort the questions below into statistical or non-statistical questions. Write the question in the appropriate box.

Statistical Question	Non-Statistical Question

 a. Fifty people at a bookstore are asked, "What is your favorite type of book?"

 b. Ten people watching a football game are asked, "How long is a football field?"

 c. Several 6th graders are asked, "What time do you usually get up in the morning?"

 d. Several people at a shopping center are asked, "How often does your family go food shopping?"

 e. Several 5th graders are asked, "What is the capital of the United States?"

CC 69

4. Which of these is NOT a statistical question?

   A Which do you prefer for breakfast, an omelet or a muffin?

   B What is your favorite food for breakfast?

   C How long does the cafeteria serve breakfast each morning?

   D How many times did you eat breakfast this week?

5. Which of these is a statistical question?

   A How many dogs are currently at the kennel?

   B How many more dogs are at the kennel now than were here last week?

   C What is the maximum number of dogs the kennel can house?

   D What is the average number of dogs staying at the kennel in the summer?

6. Sort the questions below into statistical or non-statistical questions. Write the question in the appropriate box.

Statistical Question	Non-Statistical Question

   a. Some teachers in a school district are asked, "How many school days are in the school year?"

   b. A customer asks a sales associate, "What is the difference between a smartphone and cell phone?"

   c. A student asks all of his classmates, "Do you own a smartphone or a cell phone?"

   d. A doctor asks all of his patients, "How often do you exercise?"

7. Explain why the question below is a statistical question.

A person asks many people leaving a shopping center, "How much did you spend at the shopping center today?"

Name _____

Common Core Standards Practice

6.SP.A.2 Understand that a set of data collected to answer a statistical question has a distribution which can be described by its center, spread, and overall shape.

1. The line plot below shows the number of hours per week students in a 6th grade class spend doing homework.

Number of Hours Doing Homework

Which statement is true about the data shown above? Circle all that apply.

   A The data are clustered between 4 and 6 hours.

   B There is a gap from 5 to 7 hours.

   C There is an outlier of 10 hours.

   D The range is 6 hours.

2. The table shows the number of sandwiches sold at the concession stand over the last ten weekends.

Week	1	2	3	4	5	6	7	8	9	10
Number Sold	236	186	215	192	220	242	199	218	246	210

   a. Plot the data on the number line below.

   b. Where are the data clusters?

   c. Based on the clusters, what would you expect the median to be? Explain why.

3. The line plot below shows the number of hours in one week that the members of a band practiced their musical instruments.

Number of Hours Practicing

How well does the shape of the data match a normal distribution?

4. The histogram shows the number of text messages sent by Oak High School students in one week.

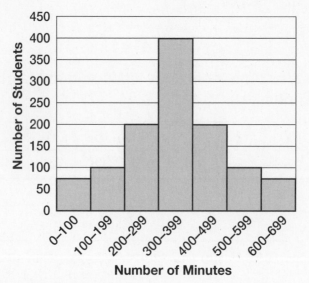

a. Describe the overall shape of the data.

b. Does the histogram show the exact mean or median of the data? Explain.

Name _____

Common Core Standards Practice

6.SP.A.3 Recognize that a measure of center for a numerical data set summarizes all of its values with a single number, while a measure of variation describes how its values vary with a single number.

1. The daily high temperatures for one week are shown in the table below.

Day	S	M	T	W	T	F	S
Temperature (in °F)	91	85	92	96	88	92	93

   a. What is the mean of the data set?

   b. How does the mean compare to the median of the data set?

2. Johanna just finished reading five books in five weeks. The five books had these numbers of pages: 208, 250, 163, 420, and 384. If Johanna wants to impress her teacher, which measure of center should Johanna use to report the average number of pages that she read each week?

3. Nafeeza records the number of bagels she sells each day in her bakery for one week.

Day	S	M	T	W	T	F	S
Dozen	24	26	24	27	20	25	38

   What is the range of the data set?

4. Janelle made a line plot that shows the number of siblings the students in her class have. Use the data in the line plot to answer the questions.

   a. What is the median number of siblings?

   b. What is the range of the number of siblings that Janelle's classmates have.

5. Use the data in the dot plot to answer the questions.

a. What is the range of scores?

b. What does the range indicate?

c. What is the median?

d. Is the median a data value? Explain.

e. What is the mean?

f. Does the mean make sense? Explain.

CC 74

Name _____

Common Core Standards Practice

6.SP.B.4 Display numerical data in plots on a number line, including dot plots, histograms, and box plots.

1. Mr. Lenz surveyed his friends to determine the number of hours they sleep per night. The data are shown in the table.

6	7	8	6	7	9	5	7
8	4	7	7	5	7	6	8

   a. Create a dot plot of the data.

   b. Determine the following values and draw a box plot for the data.

   Minimum =   Median =

   Quartile 1 =   Quartile 3 =

                          Maximum =

2. The frequency table below shows the number of hours of battery life for several different cell phones. Draw a histogram of the data.

Hours of Battery Life	Number of Cell Phones
8–10	4
11–13	6
14–16	5
17–19	3

3. The table shows the total number of home runs hit by the baseball team for the past 10 years.

36	27	23	32	30
27	24	39	63	36

Determine the following values and draw a box plot for the data.

Minimum =   Median =

Quartile 1 =   Quartile 3 =

                              Maximum =

4. The Franklin Pottery Company keeps track of the number of broken pieces of pottery per shipment. Draw a histogram of the data.

Number of Broken Pieces	Number of Shipments
0–10	2
11–20	0
21–30	4
31–40	12
41–50	10

Name _____

Common Core Standards Practice

6.SP.B.5ab Summarize numerical data sets in relation to their context, such as by: Reporting the number of observations; Describing the nature of the attribute under investigation, including how it was measured and its units of measurement.

1. Pete's Second Hand Store has several used bicycles for sale. Pete published information about the bicycles in the table shown below.

Used Bicycles for Sale

Inventory number	100	101	102	200	201	202	300	301	302
Condition	OK	OK	fair	good	good	good	very good	very good	like new
Age of bicycle (years)	N/A*	10	9	10	10	N/A*	4	3	1
Wheel diameter (inches)	22	24	24	22	21	22	20	22	24
Price	$12	$15	$18	$30	$30	$30	$85	$85	$150

*Data not available.

For each type of information in the table, write it in each of the columns that describes the type.

Can be Measured with a Tool	Depends on Someone's Judgement	Represents a Fact About a Bicycle

2. Big City Airlines flies passengers between 6 large U.S. cities. The table shows information about their schedule for the month of June.

Flight Schedule for Big City Airlines

KEY:
> **606 mi:** flight distance
> **5 flights:** number of flights, each way
> **$250:** round trip fare per passenger

	Chicago, IL	Denver, CO	Los Angeles, CA	Minneapolis, MN	New York City, NY
Atlanta, GA	606 mi 5 flights $250	1,199 mi 1 flight $300	1,945 mi 2 flights $400	907 mi 2 flights $280	764 mi 0 flights
Chicago, IL		889 mi 3 flights $200	1,746 mi 2 flights $400	349 mi 5 flights $200	727 mi 5 flights $280
Denver, CO			864 mi 0 flights	677 mi 3 flights $250	1,622 mi 4 flights $400
Los Angeles, CA				1,535 mi 2 flights $350	2,430 mi 4 flights $550
Minneapolis, MN					1,019 mi 3 flights $300

a. How many flights does the airline fly to and from Atlanta? _____

b. How many flights does the airline fly to and from Los Angeles? _____

c. Of the three types of data presented in the table, which is a measurement? What is the unit of the measurement?

d. Which data in the table might change from one month to the next? Explain why these data might change.

Name _____

Common Core Standards Practice

6.SP.B.5c Summarize numerical data sets in relation to their context, such as by: Giving quantitative measures of center (median and/or mean) and variability (interquartile range and/or mean absolute deviation), as well as describing any overall pattern and any striking deviations from the overall pattern with reference to the context in which the data were gathered.

1. A group of 12 experts each assesses the value of an antique doll. Their estimates are listed in the data table.

$50	$52	$60	$48	$59	$63
$21	$51	$95	$58	$56	$59

a. How do the mean and median of the data set compare?

b. What is the mean absolute deviation of the data set? What does it tell you about the data set?

c. What pattern do you observe in the data? What deviations, if any, do you notice in the pattern?

d. The same experts independently assess the value of an antique lamp. These estimates are shown in the table below.

$10	$120	$156	$15	$18	$140
$13	$20	$136	$17	$15	$12

The mean of this data set is $56, which was also the mean of the data set for the doll. How are the two data sets different? Consider both the measures of center and variability.

2. The Fairfield Skyliners played 15 football games this season. The table shows the points they scored in each game.

3	35	10	30	18	45	41	38
21	39	38	14	32	27	30	

a. Why is it useful to list values in order when determining measures of variability?

b. Determine these values for the data set.

Median _____   Third quartile _____

First quartile _____   Interquartile range _____

c. Describe the pattern of the data.

3. The table shows the number of customers at Julie's Restaurant during one week.

Sunday	Monday	Tuesday	Wednesday	Thursday	Friday	Saturday
290	123	150	159	190	245	390

a. What pattern do you notice in the data?

Name _____

Common Core Standards Practice

6.SP.B.5d Summarize numerical data sets in relation to their context, such as by: Relating the choice of measures of center and variability to the shape of the data distribution and the context in which the data were gathered.

1. Peter and Amy go bowling every Saturday. The table shows their scores from 6 games.

Player	Game 1	Game 2	Game 3	Game 4	Game 5	Game 6
Peter	90	75	82	66	94	67
Amy	79	81	77	79	78	80

   a. Of mean, median, and range, which statistic best explains the difference in the shape of Peter's scores and Amy's scores? Explain your answer.

   b. Peter and Amy each won half of the games they played. Is this fact better explained by comparing the means or the ranges of their scores? Explain your answer.

2. Dan and Nancy also bowl every Saturday. The table shows their scores from 6 games.

Player	Game 1	Game 2	Game 3	Game 4	Game 5	Game 6
Dan	83	86	84	50	88	87
Nancy	50	55	57	59	92	52

Compare the shape of Dan's scores with the shape of Nancy's scores. Include the concept of mean or median in your answer.

3. A scientist compares two different kinds of grasshoppers. She measures the length of 6 adults from each species. The results are shown in the table.

Species	Length (centimeters)					
A	4.3	4.1	3.9	4.5	4.3	4.2
B	1.4	4.3	2.0	3.9	1.5	2.8

   a. A science student finds an adult grasshopper that belongs either to Species A or Species B. She measures its length to be 1.8 cm. Based on the data in the table, can she determine the species? Explain your answer using the terms *mean* or *range*.

   b. A second grasshopper also belongs to either Species A or Species B. Its length is 4.2 cm. Can its species be determined? Explain your answer.

4. The table shows the number of people who live in each house on a road.

6	5	3	4	4	4	5
3	2	2	7	5	4	4

Mean: 4.14   Median: 4   Range: 5

   a. A town official thinks there is an error in the data because it is impossible for a fraction of a person to live in a house. Must the data include an error? Explain your answer.

   b. For the whole town, the mean number of people per house is also 4.14. Must the range of values for the town also equal 5 people? Explain your answer.

Name _____

Practice End-of-Year Assessment

1. **a.** Write an inequality to compare the numbers −6 and −3.

   b. Plot the two numbers on the number line shown below.

   c. Which number is to the left of the other number? Explain why it is to the left.

2. **b.** What is the coefficient of *x* in the expression shown below?

   $5 + 3x - 4y$

3. Describe a ratio of 4:1 that occurs in nature.

4. The diagram shows a three-dimensional figure. Its base is a square that measures 4 inches by 4 inches. Its four triangular sides meet at a point that is 6 inches from the midpoint of each side of the square.

Square base
4 in. x 4 in.

a. What is the name of this figure?

b. Draw the net for the figure.

c. Use the net to calculate the surface area of the figure.

5. a. What is the distance between the point *A* and point *B* shown in the graph?

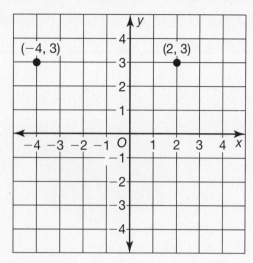

b. Tell how you found the distance.

6. Explain why the question below is a statistical question.

People leaving a movie are asked, "What did you think of the movie?"

7. Find the quotient.

$$\frac{3}{2} \div \frac{3}{8}$$

8. Draw a box plot for this set of data.

5, 10, 10, 12, 12, 15, 18, 20, 24

9. The students in art class are working with small cubes.

The teacher asks each student to assemble the small cubes into a large cube that measures n cubes on each side, with n an integer that each student chooses.

The diagram shows one example of a completed assignment, in which $n = 4$.

    a. How many small cubes are used in the figure shown above? Show how you found the answer.

    b. Write an expression for the number of small cubes used in each student's art work as a function of n.

10. Mr. Brock's bank account is overdrawn by $52. He makes a deposit of $100. Assuming he has made no other withdrawals or deposits, is his account still overdrawn? Explain your answer.

11. During the first week of July, Simon earned $65.00 for mowing lawns. This amount represents 40 percent of the total amount he earned in July.

    a. Write an equation that can be used to determine the total amount T that Simon earned in July.

    b. Solve the equation to find T. Explain what your solution means.

12. Simplify the expression below.

$26 - 3 \times 4 + 8 = \boxed{}$

13. A right rectangular prism is $7\frac{1}{3}$ inches long, $2\frac{1}{2}$ inches wide, and 6 inches tall. What is the volume of the prism?

14. Describe a real-life use for the expression $12x + 6y$.

15. A cyclist rides a 25-mile stretch of road at a constant speed. It takes her 90 minutes to ride the 25 miles. At what speed is she riding?

16. What is the greatest common factor of 64 and 80?

17. Which expression is equivalent to the expression shown below?

$2 \times (x + y) + 2 \times (x + 1)$

A $2x + 2y + 2$

B $2x + 2y - 2$

C $4x + 2y + 2$

D $2y - 2$

18. At closing time, a pizza restaurant has $5\frac{5}{8}$ pizzas still unsold. The manager divides the pizzas equally among the 3 workers to take home.

   a. Draw a model to match the problem situation.

   b. How much pizza does each worker receive?

19. Plot the following numbers on the number line.

   $-15, 45, -50, 20$

20. Alicia and Myron are bowlers. The table shows their scores for 7 games.

Alicia	70	72	74	71	72	72	73
Myron	70	60	85	74	81	65	69

How are the seven scores for each player alike? How are they different? Discuss center and variability in your answer.

21. The fare on a railroad is 40 cents for every mile of travel, plus an additional $15. Write an expression for the cost, in dollars, of a trip of n miles.

22. During one evening, a restaurant used 105 patties to make triple-stack burgers. Each triple-stack burger has 3 patties.

a. Write an equation that can be used to determine the number of triple-stack burgers the restaurant served that evening.

b. Solve the equation to find z the number of triple-stack burgers.

23. Find the product of 15.48 and 8.19.

24. Ollie sells soft drinks at a baseball stadium. The graph below shows the relationship between his sales per game and the attendance at the stadium.

According to the graph, how does attendance affect Ollie's sales?

25. Howard has a flexible pipe that is 3 feet long. He wants to use the pipe to connect a faucet to a water tank. The faucet can be moved, but the water tank is fixed in one place.

a. How far from the water tank can the faucet be? Write an inequality to represent the possible distances.

b. Represent the inequality on the number line shown here.

26. a. On the coordinate plane below, plot and label the points with coordinates (3, 4) and (−3, 4).

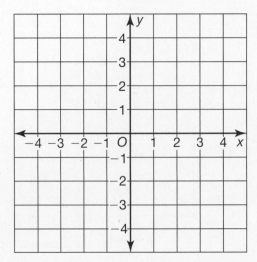

b. How do the locations of the two points differ from each other?

27. Workers pick 4,583 melons from a large field. Then they pack them into crates that hold 18 melons each. How many crates do they need to hold all of the melons? Explain your answer.

28. Which statement best describes the values of x that make this statement true?

$$|x| < 3$$

A The absolute value of x is greater than 3.

B The absolute value of x is either 0, 1, or 2.

C The difference between x and 0 is less than 3.

D The difference between x and 0 is greater than 3.

29. A trucker is 140 miles away from his destination. To arrive there in $2\frac{1}{2}$ hours, at what constant speed should he travel?

30. Which of the following are solutions to the inequality below? Circle all that apply.

$x - 5 < 9$

9	15	12
14	18	20

31. What is 1.52 less than 6.8?

32. At the library, each rack can display 6 magazines. The librarian has 72 magazines to display. How many racks does he need?

a. Write an equation that can be used to determine the number of racks the librarian needs. Use *n* to represent the number of racks.

b. Solve for *n*.

33. Dave buys 50 apples for $28. What is his cost per apple?

34. Explain why $9(t - 1)$ is equivalent to $9t - 9$.

35. Which expression is equivalent to the expression shown below?

$$z - 3 - z + z + 3$$

A 0

B z

C $3z$

D $3z + 3$

36. A figure has vertices at the points (3, 2) (3, −4), (1, −4), and (1, 2).

a. Draw the figure on the coordinate plane shown below.

b. Find the width and length of the figure.

Width: _____

Length: _____

37. Jane is taking part in a reading program. The table shows the books she has read so far.

Type of book	Number
Novels	12
History	6
Sports	3

a. What is the ratio of the number of novels to the number of sports books that Jane has read?

b. Jane reads 3 more books of each type shown in the table. What is the new ratio of novels to sports books?

38. A theater can hold 128 people. For tonight's show, 102 tickets were sold online. The remaining tickets will be sold at the ticket window. Write an inequality that can be used to determine the number of tickets available for sale at the ticket window. Then solve the inequality.

39. Fran owes $2 in library fines, and Sera owes $8 in library fines.

Write an inequality to compare the amounts that Fran and Sera owe. Use negative numbers.

40. Find the area of the triangle shown below.

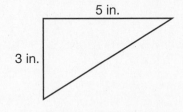

5 in.

3 in.

41. Circle the values of x that make the inequality true. (More than one value may be a correct answer.)

$x^2 < 9$

$-4 \quad -3 \quad -2 \quad -1 \quad 0 \quad 1 \quad 2 \quad 3 \quad 4$

42. Mr. Saxon has a balance of −$45 in his bank account. Then he deposits $65 into the account. Assuming he has not made any other deposits or withdrawals, is his account balance positive or negative?

43. The bait store sells 40 earthworms for $2.00. What is the price per earthworm?

44. What is the distance between the points (1,3) and (1,−2)?

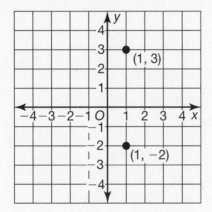

45. There are 18 players on the Boomtown Bees, a professional basketball team. The table lists the ages of each player.

24	24	25	26	30	21	27	23	22
19	24	25	22	21	24	24	24	23

Describe the shape of the age data.

46. The Freyas family studies their electricity bill and the weather report over a span of 2 years. The line graph shows their electricity use as a function of the daily high temperature.

a. When does the family pay the least for electricity?

b. When does the family pay the most for electricity?

c. From January to March, the daily high temperature gradually increases from 10°F to 50°F. How does the family's electricity bill change during this time?

d. From April to July, the daily high temperature gradually increases from 50°F to 80°F. How does the family's electricity bill change during this time?

47. Which of the values below make the equation true? Circle all that apply.

$9 + x = 12$

-4 -3 1 2 3 4

48. What is the value of 4^3?

49. The table shows the number of tournament victories this season for the 9 members of the chess team.

13	12	8	6	11	8	5	10	8

How do the mean and median of the data set compare?

50. Which expression is equivalent to the expression shown below?

$8x - 2(5 - x)$

A $6x - 10$

B $10x - 10$

C $7x - 10$

D $8x - 10$

Performance Task 1

Band Souvenirs

Part A

The Metal Pipes rock band is about to release a new album and will then go on a 20-city concert tour. They are working with an artist to create a cover for their new album, which they will also use to create T-shirts to sell at each concert venue. The artist is charging the band $2,500 to create a cover.

The band manager has received quotes from two different companies that make custom T-shirts. Both quotes include the cost of the T-shirt and the printing of the logo on it. Custom Print charges $7.50 for each T-shirt. A second company, Prince Printing, has quoted a one-time set up fee of $1,250 and $7.25 per T-shirt.

1. How much will different quantities of T-shirts cost at Custom Print and at Prince Printing? Create a table to show the cost for 2,000, 5,000, and 10,000 T-shirts at each company.

2. Which printer should the band use if they plan to have printed 5,000 T-shirts? Should they use the same printer if they plan to have printed 10,000 T-shirts? Explain your answers.

Part B

The band manager places an order for 10,000 T-shirts with the lower-cost printing company. He expects to give away 10% of the T-shirts to promote the band's new album and concert tour and will sell the rest for $15 at each concert venue.

3. How many T-shirts does the band need to sell to cover all of the costs of production?

4. How much would the band make in profit if they sold all of the T-shirts available for sale? Justify your answers.

Performance Task 2
Recruiting a Running Back

Part A

Roy and Kwame are running backs at two rival high schools in the same football league. In the table at the right are the number of yards gained per game by each of these two players during the football season.

At the end of the season, awards are given to the outstanding players in the league. Both Roy and Kwame have been nominated to win the award for best running back. The award for best running back is based on the player's game statistics.

Yards Gained per Game	
Roy	**Kwame**
97	84
68	95
125	107
188	101
116	115
85	91
45	105
108	83
146	93
60	112
118	110
92	104

1. Which player should receive the award for the Best Running Back of the Year for the league based on his game statistics? Justify your answer using measures of center (mean and median) for each player.

Part B

A college recruiter wants to offer a football scholarship to one of the two running backs. When the recruiter looks at a running back's game statistics, he looks for consistency in performance as well as the mean number of yards gained. Consistency means less variability in the data. The recruiter looks at the measures of variability for each player.

2. Based on the data in the table in Part A, who should the recruiter choose, Roy or Kwame? Justify your answer using a measure of variability, either interquartile range and mean absolute deviation. Explain your choice of measure of variability.

Name _____

Practice End-of-Year Assessment
Test 2

1. a. Write an inequality to compare the numbers −4 and −1.

b. Plot the two numbers on the number line shown below.

c. Which number is to the left of the other number? Explain why it is to the left.

2. What is the coefficient of x in the expression shown below?

$12 - 2x + 8y$

3. Walter is studying the automobiles in the school parking lot. Describe a ratio of 4:1 that might apply to his observations.

4. The figure below has a circular top and bottom. The circles both have a radius that measures 6 cm. The distance between the two circles is 8 cm.

    a. What is the name of this figure?

    b. Draw the net for the figure.

    c. Use the net to calculate the surface area of the figure.

5. a. What is the distance between the two points shown in the graph?

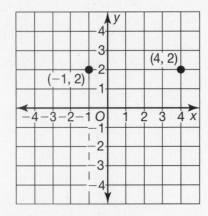

    b. Tell how you find the distance.

6. Explain why the question below is not a statistical question.
People leaving a concert were asked, "What time did the concert end?"

7. Find the quotient.

$$\frac{7}{3} \div \frac{3}{4}$$

8. The students in Mrs. Otis's class took a math test. The table shows their scores. Draw a histogram for this set of data.

74	86	65	95	97	100	77	89	94
67	77	88	78	81	84	69	79	87

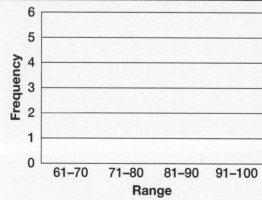

9. Students are working with small cubes. The teacher asks each student to assemble the cubes in a prism that measures s cubes on each side of the base and s cubes along the height. Each student chooses an integer s.

The diagram shows one example of a completed assignment, in which s = 3.

a. How many small cubes are used in the figure shown above? Show how you found the answer.

b. Write an expression for the number of small cubes used in each student's prism in terms of s.

10. Dr. Kane's bank account is overdrawn by $42. She makes three deposits of $50 each. Assuming she has not made other withdrawals or deposits, is her account still overdrawn. Explain your answer.

11. A dirt path leads from the highway to the Carmona ranch. Mrs. Carmona wants to pave 720 feet of the path, a length that is 60% of the total length.

    a. Write an equation that includes L, the total length of the dirt path.

    b. Solve the equation to find L.

12. Simplify the expression below.

$8 + 2 \times 9 \times 3 - 2 \times 5 = \boxed{}$

13. A right rectangular prism is $5\frac{1}{3}$ inches long, $4\frac{1}{2}$ inches wide, and 8 inches tall. What is the volume of the prism?

14. Describe a real-life use for the expression $3x + 2y$.

15. A toy car travels 15 meters at a constant speed. Its travel time is 2.5 minutes. What is the speed of the toy car?

16. What is the least common multiple of 9 and 12?

17. Which expression is equivalent to the expression shown below?

$(x + y) + 4 \times (x - 1) - y$

A $4x - 4$
B $5x + y - 4$
C $4x + 2y$
D $5x - 4$

18. The supermarket receives cereal boxes in large crates. The boxes in each crate will fill $1\frac{3}{4}$ shelves in the cereal aisle. How many crates are needed to fill 4 empty shelves?

a. Draw a model to match the problem situation.

b. How many crates are needed to fill 4 empty shelves?

19. Plot the following numbers on the number line.

50, −25

20. Benji and Chloe play miniature golf. The table shows their scores for 7 games.

Benji	30	32	31	32	30	31	31
Chloe	25	36	31	27	34	30	34

How are the seven scores for each player alike? How are they different? Discuss center and variability in your answer.

21. On Bonanza Airlines, the fee to check a suitcase is 20 cents for every pound, plus an additional $5. Write an expression for the fee, in dollars, to check a suitcase that weighs n pounds.

22. Jessie earns $9 per hour for babysitting her neighbor's kids. She earned $162 babysitting last month.

   a. Write an equation that includes h, the number of hours she babysat last month.

   b. Solve the equation to find h.

23. Find the quotient.

$367.72 \div 14.5$

24. On a TV quiz show, a team has 10 seconds to answer a question. If the team answers correctly, they receive a number of points that varies with the time, as shown in the graph.

Describe the relationship between the time that a team takes to answer the question and the points that they receive.

25. To win a trophy from the skating club, a skater must earn at least 4 points in the annual tournament.

a. Write an inequality to show the possible number of points that will win the skater a trophy. Use *x* to represent the number of points earned in the annual tournament.

b. Represent the inequality on the number line shown here.

CC 113

26. a. On the coordinate plane shown below, label the points with coordinates (2,3) and (−2,3).

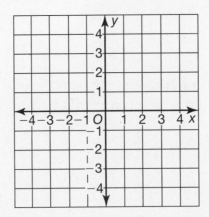

b. How do the locations of the two points differ from each other?

27. Workers pick 1,573 apples from a large orchard. Then they pack them into barrels that hold 36 apples each. How many barrels do they need to hold all of the apples? Explain your answer.

28. Which statement best describes the values of x that make this statement true?

$|x| > 9$

A x is greater than 9.

B x is less than −9.

C The difference between the absolute value of x and 0 is less than or equal to 9.

D The difference between the absolute value of x and 0 is greater than 9.

29. A trucker is 210 miles away from his destination. To arrive there in $3\frac{1}{2}$ hours, at what constant speed should she travel?

30. Which of the following are solutions to the inequality below? Circle all that apply.

$$x + 3 < 5$$

2	5	8	3	9
1	0	7	10	

31. Find the sum of 8.8 and 9.52.

32. Drew has determined that she needs to keep 7 hens for every rooster on her farm. Today she counted 84 hens.

a. Write an equation that can be used to determine the number of roosters that Drew needs to have on her farm. Use n to represent the number of roosters.

b. Solve for n.

33. José buys 50 sports cards for $4.50. What is his cost per card?

34. Which expression is equivalent to the expression shown below?

$$10k - 9 - 6k + 10$$

A $4k + 1$

B $9 - 6k$

C $20k - 15$

D $k + 4$

35. Which expression is equivalent to the expression shown below?

$$q - 7 - q - q + 10$$

A 3

B $3q$

C $3 - q$

D $q - 3$

36. A polygon has vertices at the points $(-3, -1)$, $(5, -1)$, $(-3, -4)$ and $(5, -4)$.

a. Draw the figure on the coordinate plane shown below.

b. Find the width and length of the figure.

Width: _____

Length: _____

37. Juan, a musician, plays 16 songs at a concert. The chart shows the number of each type of song.

Type of song	Number
Rock-and-roll	8
Country-western	6
Classical	2

a. What is the ratio of the number of rock-and-roll songs to the number of country-western songs that Juan plays?

b. At the next concert, Juan adds 6 more songs to increase the total to 22 songs. He adds two of each type of song listed in the table. What is the new ratio of rock-and-roll songs to country-western songs?

38. At the aquarium, the guppy tank has enough room for 85 guppies. The tank currently holds 73 guppies. What is the maximum number of guppies that the keeper can add to the tank? Write an inequality that can be used to determine the number of guppies that can be added to the tank. Then solve the inequality.

39. On Tuesday at noon, the temperature in Barrow, Alaska, was −16°C. The next day at noon, the temperature was −19°C.

Write an inequality to compare the two temperatures.

40. Find the area of the parallelogram shown below.

5 inches

3 inches

5 inches

41. For the inequality shown below, circle the values of x that make the inequality true. (More than one value may be a correct answer.)

$x^2 \geq 9$

−4   −3   −2   −1   0   1   2   3   4

42. Ms. Piper has a balance of −$35 in her bank account. Then she deposits $76 into the account. Assuming she has not made any other deposits or withdrawals, is her account balance positive or negative? Explain how you know.

43. The bait store sells 25 minnows for $4.00. What is the price per minnow?

44. What is the distance between the points (3,5) and (3,−2)? Explain how you know.

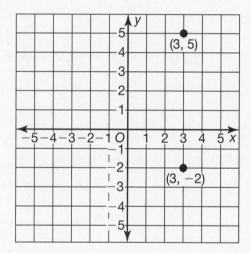

45. Nine players on the high school basketball team scored points in their most recent game. The table lists the number of points that each player scored.

11	11	8	5	3	2	2	2	1

Describe the shape of the data.

46. During recess at Fern Hill School, the children may choose to play outdoors or in the gym. The graph shows the average number of children who play outdoors as a function of the temperature.

a. When do the greatest number of children choose to play outdoors?

b. When do the fewest children choose to play outdoors?

c. From January to March, the temperature at recess gradually increases from 20°F to 40°F. How does the number of children who play outdoors change during this time?

d. From April to June, the temperature at recess gradually increases from 40°F to 70°F. How does the number of children who play outdoors change during this time?

47. Which of the values below make the equation true? Circle all that apply

$2x + 8 = 20$

-6 4 2 6 8

48. What is the value of the expression $3^3 - 1$?

49. The table shows the number of tournament victories this season for the 9 members of the chess team. The mean number of victories is 8.

Number of victories	12	11	7	5	10	7	4	8	8
Deviation from mean									

What is the mean absolute deviation of the data set? What does the mean absolute deviation tell you about the data?

50. Which expression is equivalent to the expression shown below?

$4x + 3(5 + x)$

A $3x + 15$

B $x + 15$

C $7x + 15$

D $3x + 5$

Name _____

Performance Task 3

Stadium Seats

Part A

The 4,250 seats at a high school football stadium need to be painted. The high school business manager received paint and labor estimates from two different painting crews.

Michael's Painting Crew Painting Proposal	Date	Proposal No.	Sales Rep.
	Sep 8	613	Robin

Materials

Quantity	Description	Unit Price	Total
20	Primer paint	$20.99	$410.20
40	Latex outdoor paint	$22.99	$919.60

Labor

Quantity	Description	Unit Price	Total
215	Labor	$45.00	$9,675.00

ProPainting Crew Painting Proposal	Date	Proposal No.	Sales Rep.
	September 10	122	Al

Quantity	Description	Unit Price	Total
4,250	Power washing to remove dirt and mildew	$0.35	$1,487.50
4,250	Primer coat	$0.75	$3,187.50
4,250	Two coats, latex paint	$1.50	$6,375.00

Prices quoted include all materials and labor.

1. How do the costs per seat compare between the two proposals? Tell how you determined your answer.

2. Which painting crew should the manager hire to do the work? Give at least two reasons to support your answer.

Part B

The business manager is told that the work needs to be done for the first home game of the football season, in less than two weeks. Both painting companies said they would have to add a surcharge to get the work done that quickly. Michael's Painting Crew will add a 25% surcharge to the cost of labor, while ProPainting Crew will add a 10% surcharge to total cost.

3. Which painting crew would you now recommend the manager hire to do the work? Give at least two reasons to support your answer.

Name _____

Performance Task 4
Making Towels
Part A

Mr. Angler has been contracted to make towels for the Northwoods Resort. He will make 50 hand towels, 50 bath towels, and 35 beach towels. The dimensions for each type of towel are shown in the table below.

Type of Towel	Dimensions
Hand	1 ft $\times$ $1\frac{7}{8}$ ft
Bath	$2\frac{1}{4}$ ft $\times$ $4\frac{1}{2}$ ft
Beach	3 ft $\times$ $5\frac{3}{4}$ ft

Mr. Angler will use the same terry cloth material for the hand towels and bath towels. He can get 50 yards of cloth for a very good price, which will increase his profit for this contract. The cloth is 60 inches wide.

1. Will Mr. Angler be able to make 50 hand towels and 50 bath towels with the 50 yards of cloth? If so, how much cloth will remain? If not, how much more cloth will he need?

Part B

Mr. Angler will use a less expensive terry cloth to make the beach towels. The cloth for the beach towels costs $7 per yard. It is also 60 inches wide. The cloth is sold only by the yard.

2. How much will the terry cloth for beach towels cost Mr. Angler?

Answers and Rubrics

Common Core Standards Practice

6.RP.A.1 Understand the concept of a ratio and use ratio language to describe a ratio relationship between two quantities.

1. The table shows the number and type of bagels ordered for a breakfast meeting.

Type of Bagel	Number Ordered
Plain	12
Wheat	18
Blueberry	10

   a. The ratio of plain bagels to wheat bagels is 2:3. Does this ratio represent a part-to-part or a part-to-whole ratio? Explain your answer.

     part-to-part; check students' explanations. They should note that the ratio compares plain bagels to wheat bagels, both of which are parts of the total number of bagels.

   b. The ratio of blueberry bagels to all bagels is 1:4. Does this ratio represent a part-to-part or a part-to-whole ratio? Explain your answer.

     part-to-whole ratio; check students' explanations.

2. Melinda will be going to a new school in August. Her mother tells her that the student-teacher ratio at her new school is 18 to 1.

   a. Explain to Melinda what that ratio means.

     For every 18 students, there is one teacher.

   b. Should Melinda expect to have exactly 17 classmates in her new class? Explain you reasoning.

     Sample answer: The ratio is for the entire school, so some classes may have more than 18 and some may have fewer.

   c. In her new homeroom, Melinda counts 10 boys and 14 girls (including herself). What is the ratio of girls to boys in her new homeroom? Express the ratio in two different ways.

     14 to 10 or 7 to 5; 14:10 or 7:5

page CC 1

---

3. The table shows the kinds of muffins and the number sold by a bakery on a given day.

Kinds of Muffin	Number Sold
Cinnamon	15
Blueberry	20
Apple	10

   a. Write a ratio that represents a part-to-part relationship. Explain the ratio.

     15:20, or 3:4 For every 15 cinnamon muffins sold, 20 blueberry muffins were sold.

   b. Write a ratio that represents a part-to-whole relationship. Explain the ratio.

     10 to 45 or 2 to 9; 10 out of the 45 muffins sold were apple muffins.

4. Badri is making orange juice from concentrate for breakfast. One can of concentrate is mixed with 3 cans of water. One can is equal to one cup.

   a. Which ratio represents the relationship between concentrate and water?

     Ⓐ 1:3   **B** 3:1   **C** 3:4   **D** 1:4

   b. Badri has a container that holds 2 quarts. Can he mix two cans of concentrate and water in the container? Explain your answer.

     Yes he can. 2 quarts is equal to 8 cups. To mix two cans of concentrate, Badri will use 2 cups of concentrate and 6 cups of water.

5. The students at Fields School have been asked to vote on new school hours. The two options are from 7:30 A.M. to 2:30 P.M. or from 8:15 A.M. to 3:15 P.M. The later start time won by a ratio of 2 to 1.

   a. Explain what the ratio 2 to 1 means in this context.

     Sample answer: $\frac{2}{3}$ of the students voted for the later start time and $\frac{1}{3}$ voted for the earlier start time.

   b. If 300 students voted, how many voted for the earlier start time?

     100

page CC 2

Common Core Standards Practice

6.RP.A.2 Understand the concept of a unit rate $\frac{a}{b}$ associated with a ratio a:b with b ≠ 0, and use rate language in the context of a ratio relationship.

1. Trevor rode his bicycle 25 miles in 2 hours. Assuming Trevor rode at a constant speed, how many miles did Trevor ride in one hour?

   A 4 miles

   B 5 miles

   C 10 miles

   Ⓓ $12\frac{1}{2}$ miles

2. A model dough recipe calls for 2 cups of salt, 1 cup of flour, and 2 cups of hot water. How many cups of flour are needed for each cup of salt?

   Ⓐ $\frac{1}{2}$ cup of flour

   B 1 cup of flour

   C $1\frac{1}{2}$ cups of flour

   D 2 cups of flour

3. Dong Joon and Ella have set up 180 chairs at 15 tables for the spring sports banquet. They put the same number of chairs at each table.

   a. How many chairs did they put at each table?

     12 chairs per table

   b. Write a ratio to represent the relationship between the tables and chairs.

     1 to 12 or 1 : 12 or $\frac{1}{12}$

4. Which of these ratios are rates? Circle all of the rates. Then find the unit rate for each rate.

   10 girls and 15 boys in a class

   (300 miles driven and 15 gallons used)

   20 miles per gallon

   (4 energy bars for $10)

   $2.50 per energy bar

   (21 miles biked in one hour and a half)

   14 miles per hour

   20 pine trees to 30 maple trees

page CC 3

---

5. A banana bread recipe calls for 4 cups of flour, 2 cups of mashed banana, and 1 cup of sugar. How many cups of flour are needed for every cup of banana?

   A 4 cups

   B 3 cups

   Ⓒ 2 cups

   D 1 cup

6. Mr. Hingle drove his car 300 miles on 12 gallons of gasoline. How many miles per gallon did Mr. Hingle's car get?

   A 15 miles per gallon

   B 20 miles per gallon

   Ⓒ 25 miles per gallon

   D 3,600 miles per gallon

7. Dennis and his mother went to the farmer's market to buy fruits and vegetables. The table shows what they bought at the market.

Fruit and Vegetables	Cost
Squash (3 lb)	$2.97
Tomatoes (4 lb)	$11.96
Spinach (1½ lb)	$2.25
Turnips (2 lb)	$6.50
Strawberries (3 lb)	$9.75
Blueberries (2 lb)	$7.50

   a. Find the unit rate for all of the fruits and vegetables that Dennis and his mother bought.

     Squash: $0.99/lb; Tomatoes: $2.99/lb; Spinach: $1.50/lb; Turnips: $3.25/lb; Strawberries: $3.25/lb; Blueberries: $3.75/lb

   b. Which fruit or vegetable had the highest unit rate? Which had the lowest?

     Blueberries had the highest unit rate and squash had the lowest.

   c. Can the units rates of all of the fruits and vegetables be compared? Explain.

     Yes, all of the unit rates are cost per pound.

page CC 4

Common Core Standards Practice

6.RP.A.3a Use ratio and rate reasoning to solve real-world and mathematical problems, e.g., by reasoning about tables of equivalent ratios, tape diagrams, double number line diagrams, or equations. Make tables of equivalent ratios relating quantities with whole-number measurements, find missing values in the tables, and plot the pairs of values on the coordinate plane. Use tables to compare ratios.

1. Complete the table.

Feet	1	2	3	5	10	12
Inches	12	24	36	60	120	144

2. The double number line below shows how many miles Renee biked on Sunday.

How many miles did she bike each hour?

15 mph

3. Ama's mother makes tablecloths to sell. She just bought 36 yards of material that she will use to make 12 tablecloths.

   a. Complete a table to show how much material Ama's mother needs to make different numbers of tablecloths.

Tablecloths	2	4	6	8	10	12	14
Yards of Material	6	12	18	24	30	36	42

   b. Plot the values on the coordinate grid below.

page CC 5

---

4. The table compares feet to yards.

   a. Complete the table.

Feet	Yards
3	1
6	2
9	3

   b. Plot these values as ordered pairs on the coordinate grid.

   c. How many yards equals 27 feet?

   9 yards

5. The two tables below show how much DeShawn and Sandra earn, depending upon the number of hours each works.

   a. Complete the tables.

DeShawn		Sandra	
Hours	Earns ($)	Hours	Earns ($)
1	12.25	1	11.60
7	85.75	8	92.80

   b. Compare their rates of pay. Who earns more per hour?

   DeShawn earns $12.25 per hour and Sandra earns $11.60 per hour. DeShawn earns more per hour.

page CC 6

Common Core Standards Practice

6.RP.A.3b Use ratio and rate reasoning to solve real-world and mathematical problems, e.g., by reasoning about tables of equivalent ratios, tape diagrams, double number line diagrams, or equations. Solve unit rate problems including those involving unit pricing and constant speed.

1. The table shows the prices of 3 boxes of laundry detergent of different sizes. Which size box costs the least per ounce? Explain your answer.

Size	Price
150 oz	$18.97
100 oz	$11.97
56 oz	$8.97

The 100-ounce box costs the least per ounce ($0.12 per ounce)

2. Dora and her family are driving to visit relatives. They travel 174 miles in 3 hours.

   Assuming that they are traveling at a constant speed, how many miles do they travel in one hour?

   58 mph

3. It took Trinh 4 hours to ride her bicycle 48 miles. Assuming she rode at a constant speed, how many miles did she ride per hour?

   12 miles per hour

4. Jana is going to pay $140 for 28 gymnastics lessons. Anil will pay $30 for 5 lessons.

   a. What is the rate per lesson for each?

   Jana: $5 per lesson; Anil: $6 per lesson

   b. Who is paying more per lesson? How much more?

   Anil is paying $1 more per lesson.

page CC 7

---

5. Mr. Vega is comparing the prices, shown in the table below, of 3 different jars of peanut butter. Which is the best buy? Explain.

Size	Price
18 oz	$3.28
28 oz	$4.73
40 oz	$6.44

The best buy is the 40-ounce jar, which costs $0.16 per ounce.

6. A passenger train can travel 156 miles in 3 hours. Assuming that the train travels at a constant speed, how fast does the train travel per hour?

   52 mph

7. It took Rosa 7 hours to rake 3 lawns. Assuming that the lawns are all about the same size, about how long does it take Rosa to rake one lawn?

   2 hours 20 minutes per lawn

8. Chi is going to pay $132 for 12 guitar lessons. Kele will pay $78 for 6 lessons.

   a. What is the rate per lesson for each?

   Chi: $11 per lesson; Kele: $13 per lesson

   b. Who is paying more per lesson? How much more?

   Kele is paying $2 more per lesson.

page CC 8

page CC 9

Name _____

Common Core Standards Practice

6.RP.A.3c Use ratio and rate reasoning to solve real-world and mathematical problems, e.g., by reasoning about tables of equivalent ratios, tape diagrams, double number line diagrams, or equations. Find a percent of a quantity as a rate per 100 (e.g., 30% of a quantity means $\frac{30}{100}$ times the quantity); solve problems involving finding the whole, given a part and the percent.

1. During a 30% off sale, Lourdes pays $140 for a swing set. What was the original price of the swing set?

   A $42.00
   B $182.00
   C $200.00
   D $466.67

2. The Hoboken Renegades won 40% of their 180 games. How many games did the Renegades win?

   A 72 games
   B 96 games
   C 108 games
   D 450 games

3. Rosa has a bag that contains 14 beads. The bag is 20% full. How many beads are in a full bag?
   70 beads

4. A music store ordered 400 CDs to hand out as prizes. They handed out 85% of these CDs. How many CDs did the store hand out?
   340 CDs

5. The regular price of a baseball mitt is $75. It is on sale for 25% off. What is the sale price of the baseball mitt?
   $56.25

6. Mr. Nakai wants to leave a 15% tip on a meal that cost $42.

   a. How much should Mr. Nakai leave for a tip?
   $6.30

   b. What is the total that he paid for the meal including the tip?
   $48.30

---

page CC 10

7. During a 30% off sale, Chan Hee pays $175 for a picnic table. What was the original price of the picnic table?

   A $52.50
   B $227.50
   C $250.00
   D $483.33

8. The Gilroy Garlics won 40% of their 160 games. How many games did they win?

   A 64 games
   B 96 games
   C 108 games
   D 400 games

9. Yuet is in a gymnastics class that has 4 people. The class is 25% full. How many people are in a full gymnastics class?
   16 people

10. What is 21 games out of every 100 games expressed as a percent?
   21%

11. The regular price of a softball mitt is $92. It is on sale for 35% off. What is the sale price of the softball mitt?
   $59.80

12. Mrs. Samuels wants to leave a 20% tip on a meal that cost $68.

   a. How much should Mrs. Samuels leave for a tip?
   $13.60

   b. What is the total that she paid for the meal including the tip?
   $81.60

---

page CC 11

Name _____

Common Core Standards Practice

6.RP.A.3d Use ratio and rate reasoning to solve real-world and mathematical problems, e.g., by reasoning about tables of equivalent ratios, tape diagrams, double number line diagrams, or equations. Use ratio reasoning to convert measurement units; manipulate and transform units appropriately when multiplying or dividing quantities.

1. Ayame drank 20 ounces of water in the morning, 36 ounces with lunch, and 20 ounces with dinner. How many cups of water did she drink?

   A 76
   B 9.5
   C 7.6
   D 4.75

2. A Girl Scout troop is placing markers every 16 meters along a trail. How many kilometers apart are the markers?

   A 0.016
   B 0.16
   C 1.6
   D 16

3. The length of a tennis court is 78 feet. How many inches long is the tennis court? Use equivalent ratios to find the solution.

   $$\frac{1 \text{ foot}}{12 \text{ inches}} = \frac{78 \text{ feet}}{? \text{ inches}} \quad \textbf{936 inches}$$

4. A soup recipe calls for 4 pints of chicken stock. Your measuring cup holds only one cup. How many cups of chicken stock do you need? Use equivalent ratios to find the solution.

   $$\frac{1 \text{ pint}}{2 \text{ cups}} = \frac{4 \text{ pints}}{? \text{ cups}} \quad \textbf{8 cups}$$

5. A chef made 4 liters of beef broth. She stored the broth in containers that hold 250 milliliters each. How many containers did she need? Use equivalent ratios to find the solution.

   $$\frac{1000 \text{ milliliters}}{1 \text{ liter}} = \frac{? \text{ milliliters}}{4 \text{ liters}} \quad \textbf{16 containers}$$

6. In 2010, the length of the Tour de France race course was 3,642 kilometers.

   a. How many meters long was the race?
   3,642,000 meters

   b. One mile is about 1.6 kilometers. About how many miles long was the course? Use equivalent ratios to find the solution.

   $$\frac{1 \text{ mile}}{1.6 \text{ kilometers}} = \frac{? \text{ miles}}{3,642 \text{ kilometers}}$$
   about 2,276 miles

---

page CC 12

7. A sewing club is making quilts. Each quilt is 188 centimeters long. How many meters long is each quilt?

   A 0.0188 m
   B 0.188 m
   C 1.88 m
   D 18.8 m

8. Sue Jung is training for a race. When training she drinks a lot of water. On average, she drinks $9\frac{1}{2}$ cups of water. How many ounces of water does she drink?

   A 152 oz
   B 76 oz
   C 9.5 oz
   D 4.75 oz

9. Mr. Williams wants 16,000 pounds of stone for his driveway. However, the supply company only accepts orders in tons. How many tons of stone should Mr. Williams order? Use equivalent ratios to find the solution.

   $$\frac{1 \text{ ton}}{2,000 \text{ pounds}} = \frac{? \text{ tons}}{16,000 \text{ pounds}} \quad \textbf{8 tons}$$

10. The length of a basketball court is 1,008 inches. How many feet long is a basketball court? Use equivalent ratios to find the solution.

   $$\frac{1 \text{ foot}}{12 \text{ inches}} = \frac{? \text{ feet}}{1,008 \text{ inches}} \quad \textbf{84 feet}$$

11. You are making a punch recipe that calls for 4 quarts of juice. How many cups of juice do you need? Use equivalent ratios to find the solution.

   $$\frac{1 \text{ quart}}{4 \text{ cups}} = \frac{4 \text{ quarts}}{? \text{ cups}} \quad \textbf{16 cups}$$

12. An Ironman Triathlon is made up of three different segments, as shown in the table.

Segment	Length
Swim	3.8 km
Bike	179.2 km
Run	42 km

   a. How many meters long is each segment of the race?
   3,800; 179,200; 42,000 meters

   b. If 1 mile is about 1.6 kilometers, about how many miles long was each segment of the race?
   2.4; 112; 26.25 miles

page CC 13

Name

Common Core Standards Practice

6.NS.A.1 Interpret and compute quotients of fractions, and solve word problems involving division of fractions by fractions, e.g., by using visual fraction models and equations to represent the problem.

1. Marco has $1\frac{3}{4}$ pounds of potato salad. How many $\frac{1}{8}$-pound servings of potato salad can he make?

   A 12

   B 14

   C 16

   D 24

2. Which shows the quotient of the division equation shown?

   $\frac{5}{12} \div \frac{1}{4} = \boxed{}$

   (A) $1\frac{2}{3}$

   B $1\frac{1}{2}$

   C $\frac{3}{5}$

   D $\frac{5}{48}$

3. Use a model to divide 8 by $\frac{2}{3}$. Find the quotient.

   Check students' models; 12

4. Tonya's hummingbird feeder holds $\frac{1}{2}$ cup of liquid. Tonya fills the bird feeder with a spoon that holds $\frac{1}{8}$ cup. How many spoonfuls of liquid will fill the feeder?

   a. Write an equation that can be used to solve the problem.

   $\frac{1}{2} \div \frac{1}{8} = ?$

   b. Solve the equation you wrote.

   4 spoonfuls

page CC 14

5. Find the quotient. $\frac{3}{4} \div \frac{4}{3}$.

   $\frac{9}{16}$

6. Find the quotient. $\frac{5}{11} \div \frac{1}{8}$.

   $3\frac{7}{11}$

7. Mr. Santos has $\frac{3}{4}$ gallon of paint. He thinks he has enough paint to paint 4 chairs. How much paint should he plan to use on each chair? Draw a model to match the problem, and then solve.

   Check students' models.
   $\frac{3}{16}$ **gallon**

8. The local animal shelter uses $1\frac{3}{5}$ bags of dog food each day to feed all of its dogs. For how many days will a donation of 12 bags of dog food last?

   a. Write an equation that can be used to determine for how many days the donated dog food will last.

   $12 \div 1\frac{3}{5} = \boxed{}$

   b. Solve the equation you wrote.

   $7\frac{1}{2}$; **The donated dog food will last 7 days.**

page CC 15

Name

Common Core Standards Practice

6.NS.B.2 Fluently divide multi-digit numbers using the standard algorithm.

1. Which makes the equation true?

   $1,120 \div 32 = \boxed{}$

   A 25

   B 32

   (C) 35

   D 36

2. Which makes the equation true?

   $540 \div 15 = \boxed{}$

   A 35 R10

   (B) 36

   C 36 R10

   D 42

3. Find the quotient.

   $306 \div 18 = \boxed{}$
   17

4. Find the quotient.

   $725 \div 29 = \boxed{}$
   25

5. Find the quotient.

   $11,906 \div 312 = \boxed{}$
   38 R50

6. Find the quotient.

   $5,134 \div 27 = \boxed{}$
   190 R4

7. A cyclist traveled 2,448 miles in 36 days. What was the average number of miles the cyclist traveled per day?

   68 miles

page CC 16

8. Which makes the equation true?

   $2,250 \div 125 = \boxed{}$

   A 18 R10

   (B) 18

   C 17 R 100

   D 17

9. Which makes the equation true?

   $7,128 \div 216 = \boxed{}$

   (A) 33

   B 32 R116

   C 43

   D 38

10. Solve

    $5,472 \div 152 = \boxed{}$
    36

11. Divide 9,408 by 112.
    84

12. Find the quotient.

    $9,298 \div 84 = \boxed{}$
    110 R58

13. Find the quotient.

    $6,716 \div 46 = \boxed{}$
    146

14. Jon's Clothing Store made a total of 152 sales over the weekend. The sales totaled $5,472. What was the average amount per sale?

    $36

page CC 17

Common Core Standards Practice

6.NS.B.3 Fluently add, subtract, multiply, and divide multi-digit decimals using the standard algorithm for each operation.

1. Add 2.7 + 4.25 + 3.15.
- **A** 5.85
- **B** 6.95
- **C** 7.4
- **(D)** 10.1

2. Find the quotient.

2.66 ÷ 3.5 = ☐
- **A** 0.32
- **(B)** 0.76
- **C** 0.87
- **D** 2.21

3. Find the difference.

289.37 − 283.49 = ☐

5.88 kilometers per hour

4. Multiply 22.65 × 3.82.

86.523

5. Find the quotient.

0.34)‾2.04 **6**

6. What is the product of 4.16 and 5.78?

24.0448

---

page CC 18

7. Find the sum of 15.26, 9.58, and 16.78.
- **A** 24.84
- **B** 32.04
- **(C)** 41.62
- **D** 127.84

8. Find the quotient.

185.25 ÷ 3.25 = ☐
- **A** 48
- **(B)** 57
- **C** 182
- **D** 602

9. Find the difference of $259.63 and $154.21.

$105.42

10. Multiply.

63.4
× 9.15

580.11

11. Find the quotient.

6.1)‾75.03 **12.3**

12. The San Benedetto tunnel in Italy is 4.44 km long. The Cave Ovest Tunnel in Italy is 3.79 km long.

a. Write an equation that can be used to determine the difference in length between the tunnels.

4.44 − 3.79 = ?

b. Solve the equation you wrote.

0.65 km

---

page CC 19

Common Core Standards Practice

6.NS.B.4 Find the greatest common factor of two whole numbers less than or equal to 100 and the least common multiple of two whole numbers less than or equal to 12. Use the distributive property to express a sum of two whole numbers 1–100 with a common factor as a multiple of a sum of two whole numbers with no common factor.

1. What is the greatest common factor of the numbers 12 and 54?
- **A** 2
- **B** 4
- **(C)** 6
- **D** 8

2. What is the greatest common factor of 16 and 72?
- **A** 4
- **B** 6
- **(C)** 8
- **D** 16

3. What is the greatest common factor of 80 and 95?

5

4. Find the greatest common factor of 48 and 57.

3

5. Rachel is making bouquets. She has 72 carnations and 48 roses. Each bouquet has the same number of flowers, with no flowers left over. What is the greatest number of bouquets she can make?

24

6. Adam volunteers once a month to make meals for shut-ins. He has 14 pieces of chicken and 21 pieces of corn. He needs to put the same number of pieces of chicken and corn on each plate.

a. What is the greatest number of plates he can make?

7 plates

b. How many pieces of chicken and corn will he put on each plate?

2 pieces of chicken and 3 pieces of corn

---

page CC 20

7. What is the least common multiple of 8 and 6?
- **(A)** 24
- **B** 36
- **C** 48
- **D** 52

8. Which expression is equivalent to 24 + 15?
- **A** 2 × (12 + 7)
- **(B)** 3 × (8 + 5)
- **C** 5 × (8 + 3)
- **D** 8 × (3 + 7)

9. What is the least common multiple of 6 and 9?

18

10. What is the least common multiple of 12 and 8?

24

11. Myra can set up the chairs at tables with 8 or 10 per table with no chairs left over. What is the fewest number of chairs she could be setting up?

40

12. Which expressions are equivalent to 63 + 84? Circle all that are equivalent.

9 × (7 + 9)   ⬭ 21 × (3 + 4) ⬭   3 × (21 + 84)

⬭ 7 × (9 + 12) ⬭   14 × (7 + 6)   ⬭ 3 × (21 + 28) ⬭

13. Write an expression for the area of this rectangle. Evaluate your expression to find the area.

[rectangle: 24 | 6, height 8]

(8 × 24) + (8 × 6) = 240

14. Write at least two expressions equivalent to 36 + 24.

4 × (9 + 6); 12 × (3 + 2); 6 × (4 + 6)

Common Core Standards Practice

6.NS.C.5 Understand that positive and negative numbers are used together to describe quantities having opposite directions or values (e.g., temperature above/below zero, elevation above/below sea level, credits/debits, positive/negative electric charge); use positive and negative numbers to represent quantities in real-world contexts, explaining the meaning of 0 in each situation.

1. Which of the following represents a negative number? Circle all that apply.

A deposit of $75

B an increase of 2 inches in height

Ⓒ a debt of $2

Ⓓ a loss of 5 pounds in weight

2. Temperature can be measured in degrees Fahrenheit (°F). Which of these temperatures is the coldest?

A 10°F

B 0°F

C 5°F

Ⓓ −10°F

3. Write an integer to represent 25 feet underground. Explain your answer.

−25; Check students' explanations.

4. Write an integer to represent a rise of 150 feet. Explain your answer.

+150; Check students' explanations.

5. During a football game, Howard's team gained 14 yards in one play and lost 12 yards in the next play. Write integers to represent the two plays.

+14 and −12

page CC 21

---

6. Which of the following can be represented with −8? Circle all that apply.

Ⓐ A loss of $8

B A rise of 8 feet up to sea level

Ⓒ A temperature 8 degrees below zero

Ⓓ An oil drill digging 8 miles below the surface

E A deposit of $8 in a bank account

F A change in temperature from 56°F to 64°F

7. Last week, Cy earned slightly more money than he spent. Is his net income represented by a positive number or a negative number? Explain.

A positive number. He gained money, and gain is positive.

8. A submarine travels 875 feet below sea level. Should the depth be represented by a positive number or a negative number? Explain.

A negative number. Above sea level is positive, while below sea level is negative.

9. During the day, the temperature changes from −5°F to +5°F.

a. Does the temperature become warmer or cooler?

warmer

b. Was the temperature that day ever 0°F? Explain how you know.

Yes. The temperature changed from negative to positive °F, so it must have passed through 0°F.

page CC 22

Common Core Standards Practice

6.NS.C.6a Understand a rational number as a point on the number line. Extend number line diagrams and coordinate axes familiar from previous grades to represent points on the line and in the plane with negative number coordinates. Recognize opposite signs of numbers as indicating locations on opposite sides of 0 on the number line; recognize that the opposite of the opposite of a number is the number itself, e.g., −(−3) = 3, and that 0 is its own opposite.

1. What is the opposite of $-\frac{1}{2}$?

A −2

B $-\frac{1}{2}$

Ⓒ $\frac{1}{2}$

D 2

2. Which of the following are the opposite of −5? Circle all that apply.

Ⓐ −(−5)

B $-\frac{1}{5}$

C $\frac{1}{5}$

Ⓓ 5

3. What is the opposite of 39?

−39

4. Does −(−0.7) equal −0.7 or +0.7?

+0.7

5. Place 4 and −4 on the number line.

6. a. Name two integers that are opposites.

Sample answer: −9 and 9

b. How far from 0 is each integer on a number line?

Sample answer: Each is 9 units from zero.

page CC 23

---

7. What is the opposite of $\frac{4}{3}$?

$-\frac{4}{3}$

8. Does the number −(−98) equal −98 or +98?

+98

9. What is the opposite of gaining 15 yards on a football play?

losing 15 yards

10. What is the opposite of −3.4?

+3.4

11. Place 7 and its opposite on the number line.

12. The Coulomb (C) is a unit of electric charge. Two balloons together have a total electric charge of 0 C. What could be the charges on the individual balloons? Explain your answer.

The charges must be equal in magnitude but opposite in sign. If one balloon has a charge of +2 C, the other has a charge of −2 C.

page CC 24

Common Core Standards Practice

6.NS.C.6b Understand a rational number as a point on the number line. Extend number line diagrams and coordinate axes familiar from previous grades to represent points on the line and in the plane with negative number coordinates. Understand signs of numbers in ordered pairs as indicating locations in quadrants of the coordinate plane; recognize that when two ordered pairs differ only by signs, the locations of the points are related by reflections across one or both axes.

1. In which quadrant is the point (−2, 3) located?

II

2. In which quadrant is the point (5, 8) located?

I

3. In which quadrant is the point (5, −8) located?

IV

4. In which quadrant is the point (−2, −9) located?

III

5. Match the points to their coordinates.

a. (−2, 4) _____ Point J
b. (−2, −4) _____ Point F
c. (−3, 1) _____ Point G
d. (3, 1) _____ Point H

page CC 25

---

6. How do the points (6, 9) and (−6, 9) relate to each other? Explain your answer.

The point (−6, 9) is a reflection of the point (6, 9) across the y-axis.

7. How do the points (−3, 5) and (−3, −5) relate to each other? Explain your answer.

The point (−3, −5) is a reflection of the point (−3, 5) across the x-axis.

8. How do the points (−4, 7) and (4, −7) relate to each other? Explain your answer.

The point (4, −7) is a reflection of the point (−4, 7) across both the x- and y-axes.

9. Plot all of the points that have an x-coordinate of −1 or +1, and a y-coordinate of −3 or +3.

a. In how many of the four quadrants are the points located? _____4_____

b. Why are the points each in a different quadrant?

Each point has a different combination of positive and negative signs in its coordinates.

page CC 26

Common Core Standards Practice

6.NS.C.6c Understand a rational number as a point on the number line. Extend number line diagrams and coordinate axes familiar from previous grades to represent points on the line and in the plane with negative number coordinates. Find and position integers and other rational numbers on a horizontal or vertical number line diagram; find and position pairs of integers and other rational numbers on a coordinate plane.

1. Name the integer represented by the points.

a. N −8
b. P 1
c. Q 6
d. S −3

2. Name the integer represented by the points.

a. F 5
b. G −3
c. H 9
d. J −8

page CC 27

---

3. Write the coordinates of each point.

a. M (−7, 8)
b. K (−3, 0)
c. H (6, 1)
d. O (−4, 5)

4. Plot and label each point on the coordinate grid.

a. point A at (−4, 8)
b. point B at (5, −2)
c. point C at (−7, 0)
d. point D at (3, −10)

page CC 28

page CC 29

Name _____

Common Core Standards Practice

6.NS.C.7a Understand ordering and absolute value of rational numbers. Interpret statements of inequality as statements about the relative position of two numbers on a number line diagram.

1. The statement $-8 < -2$ compares the numbers -8 and -2.

   a. Plot -8 and -2 on the number line shown below.

   b. How does the statement $-8 < -2$ explain the positions of the numbers on a horizontal number line?

   -8 is located to the left of -2 on the number line. On a horizontal number line, the lesser of two numbers is always to the left of the greater number.

2. a. Plot the numbers $|5|$ and -3 on the number line shown below.

   b. Write a statement to compare the positions of $|5|$ and -3 on the number line.

   The absolute value of a number is always positive, so 5 is located to the right of -3 on the number line. So $|5| > -3$

3. a. Plot the numbers -4 and -7 on the number line shown below.

   b. Write an inequality to compare the two numbers.

   $-7 < -4$

   c. How does the statement you wrote explain the position of the two numbers on the number line?

   -7 is located to the left of -4 on the number line. On a horizontal number line, the lesser of two numbers is always to the left of the greater number.

---

page CC 30

4. How does the statement $-38 > -77$ explain the positions of the numbers on a horizontal number line?

   -38 is located to the right of -77 on the number line. On a horizontal number line, the greater of two numbers is always to the right of the lesser number.

5. a. Plot the numbers -40 and 25 on the number line shown below.

   b. Write an inequality to compare the two numbers.

   $25 > -40$ or $-40 < 25$

   c. How are the positions of the two numbers on the number line explained by the statement you wrote?

   25 is located to the right of -40 on the number line. On a horizontal number line, the greater of two numbers is always to the right of the lesser number.

6. a. Plot the numbers -60 and -70 on the number line shown below.

   b. Write an inequality to compare the two numbers.

   $-70 < -60$ or $-60 > -70$

   c. How does the statement you wrote explain the position of the two numbers on the number line?

   -70 is located to the left of -60 on the number line. On a horizontal number line, the lesser of two numbers is always to the left of the greater number.

---

page CC 31

Name _____

Common Core Standards Practice

6.NS.C.7b Understand ordering and absolute value of rational numbers. Write, interpret, and explain statements of order for rational numbers in real-world contexts.

1. One bag of tomatoes weighs $5\frac{3}{4}$ pounds. A second bag weighs $5\frac{3}{8}$ pounds. Write an inequality to compare the weights of the two bags.

   $5\frac{3}{4} > 5\frac{3}{8}$, or $5\frac{3}{8} < 5\frac{3}{4}$

2. At the stock market, the price of Best Tea dropped $3.25 per share while the price of Yummy Tea dropped $3.33. Which company had the smaller price drop? Explain.

   Best Tea Co. had the smaller drop, because 3.25 is less than 3.33.

3. Julio and Reggie each filled a 1-liter bottle with a sports drink before their soccer game. At half time, Julio has 0.66 liter of sports drink left in his bottle and Reggie has 0.6 liter in his bottle.

   a. Who has more sports drink in his bottle? Write a number statement to explain your answer.

   Julio has more sports drink left in his bottle. 0.66 > 0.60

   b. Who drank more of his sports drink in the first half of the game? Write a number statement to explain your answer.

   Reggie drank more of his sports drink. 0.40 > 0.34

4. Four students ran the 100-meter dash. Their times are shown in the table.

Runner	Horatio	Uma	Aidan	Fiona
Time (seconds)	14.32	16.25	13.75	14.56

   a. Write the times of the students from least to greatest.

   13.75, 14.32, 14.56, 16.25

   b. Which student won the race? Explain.

   Aidan won the race. The student with the least time is the fastest runner of the group and wins the race.

---

page CC 32

5. The menu prices of a lasagna dish at several restaurants are shown below.

Restaurant	Italia	Fabio's	Maria's	Roma
Cost of Lasagna	$12.95	$12.25	$11.50	$12.99

   a. Order the costs of the dishes from greatest to least.

   $12.99, $12.95, $12.25, $11.50

   b. Which restaurant has the most expensive dish? Which has the least expensive?

   Roma has the most expensive dish; Maria's has the least expensive.

6. At 6 A.M. the temperature was $-3.2°C$. At 11 A.M. the temperature was $-2.1°C$. At 3 P.M. the temperature was $-3.7°C$. Write the temperatures from least to greatest.

   $-3.7, -3.2, -2.1$

7. The table below shows the distances in miles that 4 students live from the library.

Student	Yvonne	Stevie	Jose	Chiara
Miles from Library	$\frac{12}{5}$	$3\frac{1}{2}$	$\frac{12}{10}$	0.75

   a. List the students in order from closest to farthest away from the library. Show your work.

   In order, the distances are Chiara (0.75), Jose ($\frac{12}{10} = 1.2$), Yvonne ($\frac{12}{5} = 2.4$), and Stevie ($3\frac{1}{2} = 3.5$)

   b. Can you tell which student lives closest to Stevie? Explain.

   No. The data only show distances from the library. Stevie may or may not live on the same side of the library as any of the other students.

Common Core Standards Practice

6.NS.C.7c Understand ordering and absolute value of rational numbers. Understand the absolute value of a rational number as its distance from 0 on the number line; interpret absolute value as magnitude for a positive or negative quantity in a real-world situation.

1. Which of these has an absolute value of 5? Circle all that apply.

−10   (−5)   −0.5

15   0.05   (5)

2. What of these has an absolute value of 2.5? Circle all that apply.

5   (−2.5)   0.25

(2.5)   −0.25   1.25

3. Which numbers have a distance of 6 units from 0? Circle all that apply.

−12,   (−6)   −3,   −0.6

0.6,   3,   (6)   12

4. Which two numbers are each a distance of 8 units from 0?

A   −8 and 0
(B)   −8 and 8
C   −16 and 16
D   −16 and 0

5. What positive number has an absolute value of $\frac{2}{9}$?

$\frac{2}{9}$

6. What negative number has an absolute value of 4.25?

−4.25

7. A man dives 21 feet into the ocean from sea level. Write an expression to represent the vertical distance he travels.

−21

page CC 33

---

8. Which of these numbers has an absolute value of 3? Circle all that apply.

(−3)   6   (−$\frac{6}{2}$)

$\frac{2}{6}$ (3)   0.3

9. Which of these numbers have an absolute value of 8?

16   (−8)   ($\frac{16}{2}$)

(8) $\frac{4}{2}$ −16

10. List at least three numbers that have an absolute value of $\frac{1}{2}$.

Sample answers:
$-\frac{1}{2}$, $\frac{1}{2}$, 0.5, −0.5

11. What is the value of $-|-3\frac{1}{2}|$?

$-3\frac{1}{2}$

12. Explain why both −4 and 4 have the same absolute value.

Both are the same distance from 0 on the number line.

13. List at least 3 rational numbers that have an absolute value of 2.

Sample answers:
$\frac{4}{2}$, −2, 2, $\frac{6}{3}$, $-\frac{6}{3}$

14. A bird flew 12 meters down from a tree branch to the ground. Write an expression to represent the vertical distance the bird flew from the tree to the ground.

−12

page CC 34

Common Core Standards Practice

6.NS.C.7d Understand ordering and absolute value of rational numbers. Distinguish comparisons of absolute value from statements about order.

1. Maria withdrew $45 and $65 from her savings account.

a. Write two integers to represent the changes to the savings account.
−65 and −45

b. Which integer is greater?
−45

c. Which withdrawal changed the account more? Explain.
−65 caused the greater change because |−65| > |−45|.

2. The temperature on Monday was 6°C below zero. On Tuesday, the temperature was 11°C below zero.

a. Write two integers to represent the temperatures.
−6, −11

b. Which temperature is higher?
6°C below zero

c. Between Monday and Tuesday, did the temperature increase or decrease? Explain.
The temperature decreased. Check students' explanations.

3. Jacques and Fatima start the day at the beach, which is at sea level. Then Jacques climbs a hill that is 24 feet above sea level, while Fatima dives into the ocean to a depth of 30 feet below sea level.

a. Write two integers to represent the distances in this situation.
24, −30

b. Which integer is greater? Explain.
24 is greater than −30 because 24 is positive and −30 is negative.

c. Who had the greater vertical change in distance to sea level? Explain.
Fatima had the greater change, because |−30| > |24|.

page CC 35

---

4. Ms. Frank owes her bank $94, and she owes a neighbor $87.

a. Which number is greater, −94 or −87?
−87

b. Does Ms. Frank owe more money to the bank or the neighbor? To explain your answer, write a number statement that uses absolute value.
She owes the bank more money. |−94| > |−87|.

5. In one play of a football game, the home team lost 17 yards. In the next play, the home team gained 4 yards.

a. Write two integers to represent the amounts in the situation.
−17, 4

b. Which number is greater?
4 is greater.

c. In which play did the team's position on the field change the most? Explain your answer with a number statement that includes absolute value.
The loss of 17 yards caused the greater change. |−17| > |4|.

6. Louis and Fran are fishing on a deep lake. Louis lowers his lure to a depth of 120 feet. Fran lowers her lure to a depth of 25 feet.

a. Write two integers to represent the depths of the lures.
−120, −25

b. Which number is greater?
−25

c. Whose lure is farther from the boat? Explain your answer with a number sentence that includes absolute value.
Louis's lure is farther away. |−120| > |−25|.

page CC 36

Name _____

Common Core Standards Practice

6.NS.C.8 Solve real-world and mathematical problems by graphing points in all four quadrants of the coordinate plane. Include use of coordinates and absolute value to find distances between points with the same first coordinate or the same second coordinate.

1. a. Graph and label these points in the coordinate plane.

   A: (0, 2)   B: (−1, −3)
   C: (−2, −4)   D: (1, −1)
   E: (−1, 4)

   b. What is the distance between points B and E?
   7 units

   c. Explain how to use absolute value to find the distance between points B and E.
   Sample answer. The absolute value of point B is 3 and the absolute value of point E is 4. The distance between the points is 3 + 4 = 7

2. Judi lives at (−1, −4). To get to the library, she walks 3 blocks to the right and then 2 blocks up the coordinate grid.

   a. Graph the point where Judy lives. Label the point A.

   b. Graph the point that shows Judy's position after she walks 3 blocks to the right. Label the point B.

   c. Graph the point where the library is. Label the point C.

   d. How many blocks did Judy walk?
   5

Copyright © Pearson Education, Inc., or its affiliates. All Rights Reserved. 6

page CC 37

---

3. a. Graph (−1, −2) and (2, −2) on the coordinate plane.

   b. What is the distance between the two points?
   3 units

   c. Tell how you found the distance between the points.

   Sample answer: I found the absolute values of the x-coordinates and then added these values to find the distance.

4. a. Graph and label the points in the coordinate plane. Then draw lines to connect the points into a trapezoid.

   A: (−5, −3)   B: (2, −3)
   C: (1, 2)   D: (−4, 2)

   b. Find the distance between points C and D and the distance between points A and B.

   The distance between points C and D is 5 units; The distance between points A and B is 7 units.

5. What is the distance between (−2, 3) and (−2, −5) on the coordinate plane? Explain how you determined the distance.
   8 units; sample answer: I found the absolute values of the y-coordinates and added the values to find the distance.

Copyright © Pearson Education, Inc., or its affiliates. All Rights Reserved. 6

page CC 38

Name _____

Common Core Standards Practice

6.EE.A.1 Write and evaluate numerical expressions involving whole-number exponents.

1. Which is the value of 3^3?
   A 6
   B 9
   C 27
   D 81

2. Which is an equivalent expression for
   $0.14 \cdot 0.14 \cdot 0.14 \cdot 0.14 \cdot 0.14$?
   A $(0.14)^5$
   B 5(0.14)
   C 0.14 + 5
   D $(0.14)^{\frac{1}{5}}$

3. Evaluate the expression below.
   5^4
   625

4. Write the expression below with a single exponent.
   $\frac{1}{3} \cdot \frac{1}{3} \cdot \frac{1}{3} \cdot \frac{1}{3}$
   $$\left(\frac{1}{3}\right)^4$$

5. Which of these expressions is equivalent to 129?
   A $9^2 + 3 \cdot 4^2$
   B $7^2 \cdot 3 − 4 \cdot 7$
   C $3(2^3 \cdot 5 + 3)$
   D $5^3 + 2^2$
   E $6 \cdot 3^3 − 5 \cdot 7$
   F $2^7 + 2^0$

6. Which is the value of $\left(\frac{1}{7}\right)^2$?
   A 14
   B $\frac{1}{14}$
   C $\frac{1}{27}$
   D $\frac{1}{49}$

Copyright © Pearson Education, Inc., or its affiliates. All Rights Reserved. 6

page CC 39

---

7. Which is the value of $(0.1)^3$?
   A 0.0001
   B 0.001
   C 0.3
   D 3.1

8. Which is an equivalent expression for (5.1)(5.1)? Circle all that apply.
   A 5.1 + 5.1
   B 5.1 × 2
   C 2(5.1) × 5.1
   D 5.1^2
   E 25 + 0.1
   F $5^2 + 2 \cdot 5 \cdot 0.1 + 0.1^2$

9. Write a mathematical expression for the phrase below.
   Three more than twice the square of six
   $3 + 2 \times 6^2$

10. Write an expression with an exponent that is equivalent to the expression below.
    $\frac{1}{6} \times \frac{1}{6} \times \frac{1}{6} \times \frac{1}{6}$
    $$\left(\frac{1}{6}\right)^4$$

11. Simplify.
    $4^3 − 6 \cdot 3^2$
    10

12. Simplify.
    $3^3 − 3^2$
    18

Copyright © Pearson Education, Inc., or its affiliates. All Rights Reserved. 6

page CC 40

Name _____

Common Core Standards Practice

6.EE.A.2a Write, read, and evaluate expressions in which letters stand for numbers. Write expressions that record operations with numbers and with letters standing for numbers.

1. Which expression represents this phrase?

three times the sum of the number y and nine

A $y + 9$
B $3y + 9$
C $y + 3(9)$
Ⓓ $3(y + 9)$

2. Which expression represents this phrase?

five times of the sum of nineteen and a number k

A $5(19k)$
B $5(19) + k$
C $5 + 19k$
Ⓓ $5(19 + k)$

3. Which expression represents this phrase?

eight more than four times the number z

A $z + 8$
Ⓑ $4z + 8$
C $z + 4 \cdot 8$
D $4(z + 8)$

4. Which expression represents this phrase?

two-thirds of the sum of four and a number p

A $\frac{2}{3}(4p)$
Ⓑ $\frac{2}{3}(4 + p)$
C $\frac{2}{3}(4 - p)$
D $\frac{2}{3}p$

5. Write an expression to represent this phrase.

Five more than six times the difference of a number and eight

$5 + 6(x - 8)$

6. Write an expression to represent this phrase.

the product of twelve and six less than the number q

$12(q - 6)$

page CC 41

7. Write expressions for these phrases.

a. a number c divided by two

$\frac{c}{2}$

b. the number r less than 14

$14 - r$

c. the sum of a number x and 2 divided by 3

$\frac{(x + 2)}{3}$

d. four divided by two more than the number x

$\frac{4}{(2 + x)}$

e. the number x divided by two more than the number x

$\frac{x}{(2 + x)}$

8. Write a mathematical expression for each phrase.

a. the quotient of 11 and a number s

$\frac{11}{s}$

b. six times a number x

$6x$

c. a number w minus 7

$w - 7$

d. three times the sum of a number w and 7

$3(w + 7)$

e. six times the sum of a number x and four

$6(x + 4)$

page CC 42

Name _____

Common Core Standards Practice

6.EE.A.2b Write, read, and evaluate expressions in which letters stand for numbers. Identify parts of an expression using mathematical terms (sum, term, product, factor, quotient, coefficient); view one or more parts of an expression as a single entity.

1. How many terms are in this expression?

$4x + 3y - 12x + 5$

A 2
B 3
Ⓒ 4
D 5

2. Which statement best describes this expression?

$3x - 5y + 6x + 8 + 10y$

Ⓐ The expression is the sum of 5 terms.
B The expression is the product of 5 terms and 2 variables.
C The factors of the expression are 3, 5, 6, 8, and 10.
D The expression is the sum of the factors 3, 5, 6, 8, and 10.

3. What are the coefficients of this expression?

$10x + x - 7y + 8y$

$10, 1, -7,$ and 8

4. What is the coefficient of the r-term in this expression?

$-8r + 24s - 9r - 7$

-9

5. How many terms are in this expression?

$2x - 11x + 7$

A 2
Ⓑ 3
C 4
D 5

6. List the terms of this expression.

$-9x - 5x - 7p - 3p$

The terms are: $-9x, -5x, -7p, -3p$

page CC 43

7. $2w(w + 9)$

a. How many factors are in this expression?

3

b. What are the factors?

$2, w,$ and $w + 9$

8. Describe the parts of this expression. Use mathematical terms, such as *product*, *factor*, and *quotient*.

$\frac{x}{8} + 3y$

What is $\frac{x}{8}$? the quotient of x and 8

What is $3y$? the product of 3 and y

9. Describe the parts of this expression. Use mathematical terms, such as *product*, *factor*, and *quotient*.

$\frac{5 - x}{3} - \frac{y}{7}$

What is $\frac{5 - x}{3}$? the quotient of $5 - x$ and 3

What is $\frac{y}{7}$? the quotient of y and 7

10. List two factors of $2(x + 7)$.

2 and $x + 7$

page CC 44

page CC 45

Name _____

Common Core Standards Practice

6.EE.A.2c Write, read, and evaluate expressions in which letters stand for numbers. Evaluate expressions at specific values of their variables. Include expressions that arise from formulas used in real-world problems. Perform arithmetic operations, including those involving whole-number exponents, in the conventional order when there are no parentheses to specify a particular order (Order of Operations).

1. Evaluate the expression for $x = 10$ and $y = 3$.

$5(x - 2y)$

- **A** 10
- Ⓑ 20
- **C** 40
- **D** 50

2. Evaluate the expression $d + 15p$ for $d = 75$ and $p = 60$.

975

3. The area of a square is given by the formula $A = s^2$. What is the area of a square with a side length s of 6 in.?

$A = 6^2 = 36 \text{ in.}^2$

4. Evaluate the expression for $m = \frac{1}{4}$ and $p = -3$.

$\frac{6m}{p}$

$-\frac{1}{2}$

5. Consider the expression below.

$K = t + \frac{s}{3}$

If $t = 5$ and $s = 9$, what is the value of K?

$K = 8$

6. The formula $d = 15t$ describes the distance d in miles that Peter can ride his bike in t hours. How far does he ride in 3 hours?

45 miles

page CC 46

7. The area of a triangle is given by the formula $A = \frac{1}{2}bh$ in which b is the base of the triangle and h is the height of the triangle. What is the area of a triangle with a base of 2.5 m and a height of 1.2 m?

- Ⓐ 1.5 m²
- **B** 1.85 m²
- **C** 3 m²
- **D** 3.7 m²

8. The perimeter P of a rectangle can be calculated with the formula $P = 2l + 2w$, in which l is the length and w is the width. What is the perimeter of a rectangle with a length of 8 cm and a width of 2.3 cm?

- **A** 16 cm
- **B** 18.4 cm
- Ⓒ 20.6 cm
- **D** 23.69 cm

9. The volume of a rectangular prism is given by the formula $V = l \times w \times h$. What is the volume of a rectangular prism with a length of 10 cm, a width of $6\frac{1}{2}$ cm, and a height of $2\frac{1}{4}$ cm?

$V = 146\frac{1}{4} \text{ cm}^3$

10. Consider the expression below.

$2t + 4w$

Evaluate the expression for $t = 3$ and $w = 0.2$.

6.8

11. Consider the expression below.

$\frac{3x + 2y}{4}$

Evaluate the expression for $x = 2$ and $y = 0.5$.

$\frac{7}{4}$ or $1\frac{3}{4}$

12. Evaluate the expression for $f = 5$ and $g = 11$.

$3f + 2g - 16$

21

page CC 47

Name _____

Common Core Standards Practice

6.EE.A.3 Apply the properties of operations to generate equivalent expressions.

1. Which expression is equivalent to $3(x + 5)$?

- **A** $3x + 5$
- Ⓑ $3x + 15$
- **C** $x + 15$
- **D** $x + 8$

2. Which expression is equivalent to $2(3v + 7)$?

- **A** $6v - 7$
- **B** $3v + 14$
- Ⓒ $6v + 14$
- **D** $6v + 7$

3. Which property can be used to show that $4r + 3s + 2r = 6r + 3s$? Explain your answer.

Associative or Commutative Property; check students' explanations.

4. Explain why $2(3t - w)$ is equivalent to $6t - 2w$.

Check students' explanations. Sample answer: The distributive property states that you can multiply each addend by the value, so $2(3t - w) = (2 \times 3t) - (2 \times w) = 6t - 2w$.

5. How are these two sets of equivalent expressions similar?

$24 + 84 = 12(2 + 7)$ $5 + 10x = 5(1 + 2x)$

Both sets of expressions use the distributive property to generate an equivalent expression.

6. a. Write an expression equivalent to $3w - 3w + 3w$ with just one term.

$3w$

b. What property or properties applies?

Check students' answers; possible answers: identity property of addition or commutative property.

7. Jorge says that $4(x + 3) + 5$ is equal to $4x - 17$. Is he right? Explain your answer.

No, the equivalent expression is 4x + 17.

page CC 48

8. Which expression is equivalent to $3y + 3y + 3y + 3y$?

- Ⓐ $12y$
- **B** $81y$
- **C** $3y^4$
- **D** $6y$

9. Which expression is equivalent to $15m + 18$?

- **A** $15m - 18$
- **B** $5m + 18$
- **C** $5m + 6$
- Ⓓ $3(5m + 6)$

10. Use the distributive property to write an expression equivalent to $7(9x - 5)$.

$63x - 35$

11. How are these two sets of equivalent expressions similar?

$76 + 102 + 24 = (76 + 24) + 102$ $2x + 3y - 12 + x = (2x + x) + 3y - 12$

Both sets of expressions use the associative property to regroup terms to make it easier to simplify the expression.

12. Markie wrote these expressions on the board.

$8(0.3x + 2.6) = 2.4x + 20.8$

Is Markie's work correct? Explain your answer.

Yes, Markie used the distributive property appropriately and correctly multiplied decimals.

13. Explain why $x + y + x + y$ is equivalent to $2x + 2y$.

Check students' explanations. Sample answer: The associative property states that you can regroup like terms in an expression.

14. Which property can be used to show that $4r + 12s + 20t = 4(r + 3s + 5t)$? Explain your answer.

Distributive Property; check students' explanations.

Common Core Standards Practice

6.EE.A.4 Identify when two expressions are equivalent (i.e., when the two expressions name the same number regardless of which value is substituted into them).

1. Which expression is equivalent to $5s + 4$?

   A $4(s + 1)$
   B $9s$
   C $5(s + 1)$
   Ⓓ $s + s + s + s + s + 4$

2. Which expression is equivalent to the expression below?

   $42r - 42$

   A $7(r - 6)$
   B $6(r - 7)$
   C $41r$
   Ⓓ $42(r - 1)$

3. Simplify $x - 3x + (9 - 2) + 5x$.

   $3x + 7$

4. Simplify $y + 7y - (3y + 7)$.

   $5y - 7$

5. Which of these expressions is equivalent to $3g + 21$? Circle all that apply.

   ⟨$3(g + 7)$⟩ $3(g - 7)$ $3(g + 21)$ $3(g - 21)$

6. Which of these expressions is equivalent to $w + w - w + 6$? Circle all that apply.

   $3w + 6$ ⟨$w + 6$⟩ $3 + 3 - (3 - w)$ $w - 6$

page CC 49

---

7. Find the expression that is equivalent to the expression below.

   $3(2d - 5)$

   A $-15 - 6d$
   B $15 - 2d$
   C $6d + 15$
   Ⓓ $6d - 15$

8. Find the expression that is equivalent to the expression below.

   $6y + (2y - 3) + 6$

   A $12y - 3$
   B $8y - 9$
   C $4y + 3$
   Ⓓ $8y + 3$

9. Simplify the expression.

   $(5 + 2x) + (2x + 6) + 1$

   $4(x + 3)$

10. Simplify the expression.

   $4g + 5 - g - g + 2 + g$

   $7 + 3g$

11. Write the expression $6x - 8$ as the product of 2 and another factor.

   $2(3x - 4)$

12. Write the expression $15 - 5y$ as the product of 5 and another factor.

   $5(3 - y)$

13. Write the expression $4x + 8$ as the product of 4 and another factor.

   $4(x + 2)$

page CC 50

Common Core Standards Practice

6.EE.B.5 Understand solving an equation or inequality as a process of answering a question: which values from a specified set, if any, make the equation or inequality true? Use substitution to determine whether a given number in a specified set makes an equation or inequality true. Which value of *t* makes the inequality true?

1. Which values of *t* make the inequality true? Circle all that apply.

   $4t - 1 < 12$

   ①   6   4
   5   ③   ②

2. Which values of *w* make the inequality true? Circle all that apply.

   $5w - 1 > 17$

   ⑧   ⑥   ④
   ⑤   3   2

3. Which values of *t* make the inequality true? Circle all that apply.

   $t + 6 \leq 14$

   10   ⑤   ⑧
   15   12   ⑦

4. Which values for *m* from the set $\{3, 5, 7\}$ make the inequality true?

   $5m - 6 < 20$

   3 and 5

5. Which value from the set $\{2, 6, 8\}$ makes $3x - 5 = 13$ true?

   6

6. Which values for *m* from the set $\{\frac{1}{2}, \frac{1}{10}, \frac{1}{5}\}$ make the inequality true?

   $2m \geq \frac{1}{10}$

   $\frac{1}{2}, \frac{1}{5}, \frac{1}{10}$

7. Is 5 a solution to the inequality below? Explain how you know.

   $x - 3 > 2$

   No, 5 is not a solution. $5 - 3$ equals 2, so it is not greater than 2.

8. Is 12 a solution to the inequality below? Explain how you know.

   $24 - y \leq 12$

   Yes, it is a solution. $24 - 12 = 12$ so that makes the inequality true.

page CC 51

---

9. Which values for *t* make the inequality true?

   $35 - 4t > 7$

   8   ⑥   ④
   7   10   9

10. Which value for *x* makes the equation true?

   $x + \frac{1}{8} = \frac{3}{4}$

   A $\frac{1}{2}$
   Ⓑ $\frac{5}{8}$
   C $\frac{3}{4}$
   D 1

11. Which values for *x* from the set $\{2, 4, 6\}$ make the inequality true?

   $25 - 4x < 3$

   6

12. Which value for *a* from the set $\{0, 5, 9\}$ makes the equation true?

   $a + 5 = 14$

   9

13. Which values for *g* from the set $\{0.4, 0.2, 0.6\}$ make the equation true?

   $5g = 1$

   0.2

14. Which values for *y* make the inequality true?

   $0.2y > 1$

   A 0.5
   B 5
   Ⓒ 7
   Ⓓ 10

15. Is 7 a solution to the equation below? Explain how you know.

   $2y + 3 = 20$

   No, it is a solution. $14 + 3 = 17$, not 20.

16. Is 8 a solution to the inequality below? Explain how you know.

   $3x - (4 + x) \geq 12$

   Yes, it is a solution. $24 - 12 = 12$ so that makes the inequality true.

page CC 52

page CC 53

Name _____

Common Core Standards Practice

6.EE.B.6 Use variables to represent numbers and write expressions when solving a real-world or mathematical problem; understand that a variable can represent an unknown number, or, depending on the purpose at hand, any number in a specified set.

1. Chi has five fewer than twice as many markers as Rosa. Rosa has x markers. Which expression represents the number of markers that Chi has?

   A $(5 + 2)x$
   B $2x - 5$
   C $2x + 5$
   D $x + 5 - 2$

2. Juanita earns money by mowing lawns. She charges each customer $8 for expenses plus $12 per hour. Which expression can be used to determine how much Juanita earns mowing a lawn for h hours?

   A $12h + 8$
   B $12h - 8$
   C $8h + 12$
   D $8h - 12$

3. At a school carnival, Jasmine paid $5 for admission and $1.25 per ride. Write an algebraic expression to represent the total amount Jasmine spent in dollars if she went on t rides.

   $5 + 1.25t$

4. Mato had 18 video games. He won g video games in a contest. Write an algebraic expression for the number of video games that Mato has now.

   $18 + g$

5. Marita has $100 to buy new clothes. She wants to buy a pair of jeans for $35 and some tops that each cost $27. Her older sister tells her she can use the equation $100 - 35 = 27t$ to determine how many tops she can buy.

   a. What does t represent in the equation?
   the number of tops Marita can buy

   b. Is Marita's sister correct? Explain.
   Yes. Check students' explanations.

page CC 54

Match the expressions to the situation. Some expressions may not match any situation. Some may match more than one situation.

6. a. Kelsey has three more than five times the number of seashells Hahn has.

   b. A county fair charges each attendee $15 for admission and $2.00 per ride ticket.

   c. An appliance repairman charges $65 per hour plus a service fee of $15.

   d. Emilio bought a skateboard and a helmet. He spent $65 on the skateboard and some money for the helmet.

   e. Rana had $15 at the start of week. During the week, she bought two songs online.

   $65h + 15$

   $65 + h$

   $15 + 2t$

   $5x + 3$

   $3w - 5$

7. Mrs. Andrews sent Phil and Frank to the store with $20. They need to buy bread that costs $3.50, and a dozen eggs that cost $2. The two boys can spend the rest of the money on snacks that cost $1.50 each. Phil says they can use the equation $20 - (3.50 - 2) = 1.5s$ to determine how many snacks they can buy.

   a. What does s represent in the equation?
   the number of snacks they can buy

   b. Is Phil correct? Explain.
   No. The equation should be $20 - (3.5 + 2) = 1.5s$.

page CC 55

Name _____

Common Core Standards Practice

6.EE.B.7 Solve real-world and mathematical problems by writing and solving equations of the form $x + p = q$ and $px = q$ for cases in which p, q, and x are all nonnegative rational numbers.

1. Gabriela spent $83.97 on three jackets. Each jacket cost the same amount. Write an algebraic equation to show the cost of one jacket. Solve the equation.

   $3x = 83.97$;
   $x = 27.99$;

2. Yomi has a job shoveling snow. She charges $18 for each driveway shoveled. One winter day she made $108. Write an equation to show the number of driveways she shoveled. Solve the equation.

   $18d = 108$, $d = 6$

3. Chan Hee is paid $25 for tutoring. Then he spends $4 on a sandwich and $2 on a drink. Write an equation to show the amount of money Chan Hee has now. Solve the equation.

   $4 + 2 + x = 25$;
   $x = 19$

4. A school spent $149.25 on baseballs. Each baseball cost $1.99. Write an equation to show the number of baseballs purchased by the school. Solve the equation.

   $1.99b = 149.25$;
   $b = 75$

5. Tell how to solve for w. Then solve.
   $w + 1\frac{1}{3} = 6$

   subtract $1\frac{1}{3}$ from both sides of the equation; $w = 4\frac{2}{3}$

6. Tell how to solve for h. Then solve.
   $h - \frac{3}{5} = \frac{7}{4}$

   add $\frac{3}{5}$ to both sides of the equation; find a common denominator; $h = 2\frac{7}{20}$

page CC 56

7. Tell how to solve for t. Then solve.
   $t + 2.34 = 6.89$

   subtract 2.34 from both sides of the equation; $t = 4.55$

8. Solve. $y - 1\frac{1}{4} = 8\frac{1}{2}$

   add $1\frac{1}{4}$ to both sides of the equation; find a common denominator; $y = 9\frac{3}{4}$

9. Sophia spent $33.40 on four bracelets. Each bracelet cost the same amount. Write an equation to show the cost of one bracelet. Solve the equation.

   $4x = 33.40$;
   $x = 8.35$

10. Lakeisha has a babysitting job. She charges $7 per hour. One week she earned $168. Write an equation to show the number of hours Lakeisha babysat that week. Solve the equation.

   $7h = 168$; $h = 24$

11. Anton won $30 for running in a race. He spends $12 on a shirt and $6 on lunch. Write an equation to show the amount of money Anton has left. Solve the equation.

   $12 + 6 + x = 30$;
   $x = 12$

12. A summer recreation league has 72 girls signed up for softball. Each softball team has 12 players. Write an equation to show the number of teams that could be formed. Solve the equation.

   $12b = 72$; $b = 6$

page CC 57

Name _____

Common Core Standards Practice

6.EE.B.8 Write an inequality of the form x > c or x < c to represent a constraint or condition in a real-world or mathematical problem. Recognize that inequalities of the form x > c or x < c have infinitely many solutions; represent solutions of such inequalities on number line diagrams.

1. A table can seat at most 8 people. Represent the number of people who can sit at the table as an inequality.

$X \leq 8$

2. A package of pasta states to cook the pasta for up to 11 minutes.

   a. Represent this as an inequality.

   $X \leq 11$

   b. What are some possible numbers of minutes the pasta can cook?

   a positive number less than or equal to 11: 3, 8, 9.5

3. A roller coaster rider must be at least 54 inches tall.

   a. Represent the height of a roller coaster rider as an inequality.

   $X \geq 54$

   b. Graph the inequality on the number line.

   50 52 54 56 58 60

4. Campers are told to bring at least 10 pairs of socks for a camping trip.

   a. Represent the numbers of pairs of socks as an inequality.

   $X \geq 10$

   b. What are some possible numbers of pairs of socks a camper would bring?

   any integer greater than or equal to 10: 10, 11, 12, etc.

5. A cell phone plan offers up to 700 free minutes every month.

   a. Represent the number of free minutes as an inequality.

   $X \leq 700$

   b. Graph this inequality on a number line.

   680 690 700 710 720

page CC 58

6. The altitude of a plane must always be no less than 200 feet above ground except during take off and landing.

   a. Represent the flying altitude of the plane as an inequality.

   $X \geq 200$

   b. Graph the inequality on the number line.

   0   50   100   150   200   250   300   350

   c. How many solutions does this inequality have? Explain your answer.

   an infinite number

7. Match the inequality to the situation. Some situations may not match to an inequality.

   a. DeShawn reads at least 3 books each month.

   b. A soccer team roster can have no more than 20 active players.

   c. Angie puts at least 6 flowers in each flower arrangement.

   d. Riders of this ride must be over 35 inches tall.

   e. Maya can invite no more than 15 people to her party.

   x > 35
   x ≤ 20
   x ≥ 3
   x < 20
   x ≥ 6

8. Classes at Jonas' school can not have more than 15 students. Graph this inequality on a number line.

   0   2   4   6   8   10   12   14   16   18

page CC 59

Name _____

Common Core Standards Practice

6.EE.C.9 Use variables to represent two quantities in a real-world problem that change in relationship to one another; write an equation to express one quantity, thought of as the dependent variable, in terms of the other quantity, thought of as the independent variable. Analyze the relationship between the dependent and independent variables using graphs and tables, and relate these to the equation.

1. What is the relationship between the two variables?

x	y
1	4.5
2	9
3	13.5
4	18

$y = 4.5x$; when x increases by 1, y increases by 4.5.

2. Complete the table.
   $y = 3x - 2$

x	y
1	1
2	4
3	7
4	10

3. Use the graph to describe the change in y as x increases by 1.

   For every increase in x by 1, y increases by 2.

page CC 60

4. Write an equation that represents the relationship between the two variables.

x	1	2	3	4
y	9	16	23	30

$y = 7x + 2$

5. The number of baseball cards in an album, c, depends on the number of pages, p. The equation $c = 9p$ is used to determine the number of cards. Complete the table.

p	c
1	9
2	18
8	72

6. A cable company charges $25 per month and $5 for every pay-per-view movie ordered.

   a. Write the equation that represents the situation. Let B represent the total bill and m represent the number of pay-per-view movies.

   $B = 5m + 25$

   b. Complete the table.

m	B
1	30
2	35
3	40
8	65

   c. Graph the solution.

page CC 61

Common Core Standards Practice

6.G.A.1 Find the area of right triangles, other triangles, special quadrilaterals, and polygons by composing into rectangles or decomposing into triangles and other shapes; apply these techniques in the context of solving real-world and mathematical problems.

1. Which is the area of a triangle with base length 6 units and height 9 units?

- A 3 square units
- B 15 square units
- Ⓒ 27 square units
- D 54 square units

2. Find the area of the parallelogram.

- A 12 in.²
- B 24 in.²
- C 28 in.²
- Ⓓ 32 in.²

3. a. Compose the right triangle into a rectangle.

b. Explain how to use the composed rectangle to find the area of the triangle.

The triangle is half the size of the rectangle, so divide the area of the rectangle in half to find the area of the triangle.

4. a. Decompose the trapezoid into rectangles and/or triangles.

 Answers may vary.

b. Find the areas of the shapes you used in part (a).

Answers may vary. Sample: area of each triangle = 10.5 cm², area of rectangle = 63 cm²

c. Find the area of the trapezoid.

84 cm²

CC 61 Copyright © Pearson Education, Inc., or its affiliates. All Rights Reserved. 6

---

page CC 62

5. What is the area of the figure?

93 in.²

6. Fujita is making a pennant. How much material does he need to make the pennant?

31.5 ft²

7. A company is making a tile design. Each tile is an 8-in. by 8 in. square. How many triangular pieces shown below fit inside each square tile?

16 triangular pieces

8. The floor of a work shed has the shape of a trapezoid as shown. What is the area of the floor?

72 ft²

CC 62 Copyright © Pearson Education, Inc., or its affiliates. All Rights Reserved. 6

---

page CC 63

Common Core Standards Practice

6.G.A.2 Find the volume of a right rectangular prism with fractional edge lengths by packing it with unit cubes of the appropriate unit fraction edge lengths, and show that the volume is the same as would be found by multiplying the edge lengths of the prism. Apply the formulas $V = lwh$ and $V = bh$ to find volumes of right rectangular prisms with fractional edge lengths in the context of solving real-world and mathematical problems.

1. A flower box has the shape of a rectangular prism and is 3 ft long, $2\frac{1}{2}$ ft wide, and $\frac{1}{2}$ ft deep. How many cubic feet of potting soil will it hold?

- A $1\frac{1}{2}$ ft³
- Ⓑ $3\frac{3}{4}$ ft³
- C 6 ft³
- D $7\frac{1}{2}$ ft³

2. A rectangular prism has a length of $10\frac{1}{3}$ in., a width of 6 in., and a height of $9\frac{1}{4}$ in.

a. Draw a diagram of the prism.

Answers may vary. Sample:

b. Determine the volume of the rectangular prism.

$573\frac{1}{2}$ in.³

3. Marcus is packing a large box with some small boxes. The large box has the shape of a rectangular prism and is $2\frac{1}{2}$ ft long, $1\frac{1}{2}$ ft wide, and 2 ft tall. Each small box is cube-shaped with a side length of $\frac{1}{2}$ ft. How many of the small boxes will fit in the large box?

60 small boxes will fit in the large box.

CC 63 Copyright © Pearson Education, Inc., or its affiliates. All Rights Reserved. 6

---

page CC 64

4. A rectangular swimming pool is 25 ft long and $20\frac{1}{2}$ ft wide, and it must be filled to a depth of $4\frac{1}{2}$ ft. One cubic foot of water is equal to $7\frac{1}{2}$ gallons. How many gallons of water will it take to fill the pool?

$17,296\frac{7}{8}$ gallons

5. Jaipal is making a small planter box. The box is $\frac{1}{2}$ foot long, $\frac{2}{3}$ foot wide, and $\frac{7}{8}$ foot deep. Jaipal has $\frac{1}{4}$ cubic foot of potting soil. Will the potting soil fit in the planter? Explain.

Yes: the planter can hold $\frac{7}{24}$ cubic foot, which is slightly larger than the amount of potting soil.

6. Which is the volume of the rectangular prism shown below?

- A $\frac{3}{32}$ cubic yard
- Ⓑ $\frac{7}{32}$ cubic yard
- C $2\frac{1}{2}$ cubic yards
- D 5 cubic yards

7. A fish tank has the following dimensions: $24\frac{1}{2}$ in. long, $12\frac{1}{2}$ in. wide, and $12\frac{3}{4}$ in. tall. What is the volume of the fish tank?

$3,904\frac{11}{16}$ in.³

CC 64 Copyright © Pearson Education, Inc., or its affiliates. All Rights Reserved. 6

page CC 65

Name _____

Common Core Standards Practice

6.G.A.3 Draw polygons in the coordinate plane given coordinates for the vertices; use coordinates to find the length of a side joining points with the same first coordinate or the same second coordinate. Apply these techniques in the context of solving real-world and mathematical problems.

1. A graphic designer is making letters for a varsity jacket. He is drawing the letters on a coordinate grid. One of the letters has the following vertices: $(4, -1)$, $(4, -3)$, $(-2, -3)$, $(-2, 5)$, $(0, 5)$, $(0, -1)$

   Plot the points and connect them to form a polygon. What letter is formed?

   The letter L is formed.

2. **a.** What is the distance from point A to point B?

   6 units

   b. What is the distance from point B to point C?

   5 units

3. Mia draws a map of her city on a coordinate grid. The park is located at $(-3, 2)$, the library is located at $(1, 2)$, and Mia's home is located at $(1, -1)$.

   a. Plot the locations on a coordinate grid. Each unit on the grid represents 1 mile.

   b. What shape is formed by joining the three points?

   a right triangle

   c. What is the distance from the park to the library?

   4 mi

   d. What is the distance from the library to Mia's house?

   3 mi

page CC 66

4. The following coordinates are the vertices of a polygon: $(2, 1)$, $(2, 7)$, $(7, 7)$, and $(7, 1)$.

   a. Plot the points and connect them to form a polygon.

   b. What is the perimeter of the polygon?

   22 units

5. Rectangle $ABCD$ has vertices $A(1\frac{1}{2}, 8)$, $B(6\frac{1}{2}, 8)$, $C(6\frac{1}{2}, 2\frac{1}{2})$, and $D(1\frac{1}{2}, 2\frac{1}{2})$.

   a. Plot the points on a coordinate grid.

   b. Which sides of the rectangle are longest? Explain how you know.

Sides AD and BC are the longest sides of the rectangle because $AD = BC = 5\frac{1}{2}$ units and $AB = DC = 5$ units.

page CC 67

Name _____

Common Core Standards Practice

6.G.A.4 Represent three-dimensional figures using nets made up of rectangles and triangles, and use the nets to find the surface area of these figures. Apply these techniques in the context of solving real-world and mathematical problems.

1. Which net will form a cube?

   A

   B

   C

   Ⓓ

2. Draw a net for a rectangular prism.

   Answers may vary. Sample:

3. A cereal box in the shape of a rectangular prism has the dimensions shown below.

   15 in.

   12 in.   3 in.

   a. Draw a net of the cereal box and label the dimensions.

   Answers may vary. Sample:

   15 in.

   3 in.   3 in.   12 in.

   12 in.

   b. Calculate the surface area of the cereal box.

   522 in.²

page CC 68

4. Describe the shapes of the faces that are needed to construct a square pyramid and then draw a net of this figure.

   1 square base and 4 triangular faces

   Answers may vary. Sample:

5. Which figure will the given net form?

   Ⓐ

   B

   C

   D

6. A movie theater is designing a new container for its popcorn. The new container has the shape of a rectangular pyramid as shown below.

   12 in.

   10 in.   8 in.

   a. Draw a net of the new container.

   Answers may vary. Sample:

   8 in.

   12 in.   10 in.

   b. Calculate the surface area of the container.

   320 in.²

   c. The company that makes the containers charges $.02 per square inch of container material. How much will 500 containers cost?

   $3,200

page CC 69

Name _____

Common Core Standards Practice

6.SP.A.1 Recognize a statistical question as one that anticipates variability in the data related to the question and accounts for it in the answers.

1. Which of these is a statistical question?

   A You ask a friend, "When is your birthday?"

   Ⓑ You ask several people, "In what year were you born?"

   C You ask all of your friends, "What year is this?"

   D You ask a parent, "What time is it?"

2. Which of these is a NOT statistical question?

   A You ask a friend, "What movie do you want to see?"

   B You ask your friends, "Did you see the latest Transformers movie?"

   C You ask many of your classmates, "Which Harry Potter movie did you like best?"

   Ⓓ You ask several people, "What did you think of the movie you just saw?"

3. Sort the questions below into statistical or non-statistical questions. Write the question in the appropriate box.

Statistical Question	Non-Statistical Question
What is your favorite type of book?	How long is a football field?
What time do you usually get up in the morning?	What is the capital of the United States?
How often does your family go food shopping?	

   a. Fifty people at a bookstore are asked, "What is your favorite type of book?"

   b. Ten people watching a football game are asked, "How long is a football field?"

   c. Several 6th graders are asked, "What time do you usually get up in the morning?"

   d. Several people at a shopping center are asked, "How often does your family go food shopping?"

   e. Several 5th graders are asked, "What is the capital of the United States?"

page CC 70

4. Which of these is NOT a statistical question?

   A Which do you prefer for breakfast, an omelet or a muffin?

   B What is your favorite food for breakfast?

   Ⓒ How long does the cafeteria serve breakfast each morning?

   D How many times did you eat breakfast this week?

5. Which of these is a statistical question?

   A How many dogs are currently at the kennel?

   B How many more dogs are at the kennel now than were here last week?

   C What is the maximum number of dogs the kennel can house?

   Ⓓ What is the average number of dogs staying at the kennel in the summer?

6. Sort the questions below into statistical or non-statistical questions. Write the question in the appropriate box.

Statistical Question	Non-Statistical Question
Do you own a smartphone or a cell phone?	What is the difference between a smartphone and cell phone?
How often do you exercise?	How many school days are in the school year?

   a. Some teachers in a school district are asked, "How many school days are in the school year?"

   b. A customer asks a sales associate, "What is the difference between a smartphone and cell phone?"

   c. A student asks all of his classmates, "Do you own a smartphone or a cell phone?"

   d. A doctor asks all of his patients, "How often do you exercise?"

7. Explain why the question below is a statistical question.

   A person asks many people leaving a shopping center, "How much did you spend at the shopping center today?"

   The question will lead to answers with different numerical values.

page CC 71

Name _____

Common Core Standards Practice

6.SP.A.2 Understand that a set of data collected to answer a statistical question has a distribution which can be described by its center, spread, and overall shape.

1. The line plot below shows the number of hours per week students in a 6th grade class spend doing homework.

   Number of Hours Doing Homework

   Which statement is true about the data shown above? Circle all that apply.

   Ⓐ The data are clustered between 4 and 6 hours.

   B There is a gap from 5 to 7 hours.

   Ⓒ There is an outlier of 10 hours.

   D The range is 6 hours.

2. The table shows the number of sandwiches sold at the concession stand over the last ten weekends.

Week	1	2	3	4	5	6	7	8	9	10
Number Sold	236	186	215	192	220	242	199	218	246	210

   a. Plot the data on the number line below.

   b. Where are the data clusters?

   between 185 and 200, between 210 and 220, and from 235 to 250

   c. Based on the clusters, what would you expect the median to be? Explain why.

   Check students' estimates and explanations. The estimate should be between 215 and 225 because it is the middle cluster and the median is a measure of center.

page CC 72

3. The line plot below shows the number of hours in one week that the members of a band practiced their musical instruments.

   Number of Hours Practicing

   How well does the shape of the data match a normal distribution?

   Students should note that although the distribution is somewhat skewed, it is fairly close to a normal distribution.

4. The histogram shows the number of text messages sent by Oak High School students in one week.

   a. Describe the overall shape of the data.

   The histogram is symmetrical: It has the same shape on either side of the center range of 300–399.

   b. Does the histogram show the exact mean or median of the data? Explain.

   No. The histogram shows that the mean or median is between 300 and 399 minutes, but does not show the exact value.

Page CC 73

Name _____

Common Core Standards Practice

6.SP.A.3 Recognize that a measure of center for a numerical data set summarizes all of its values with a single number, while a measure of variation describes how its values vary with a single number.

1. The daily high temperatures for one week are shown in the table below.

Day	S	M	T	W	T	F	S
Temperature (in °F)	91	85	92	96	88	92	93

   a. What is the mean of the data set? **91°F**

   b. How does the mean compare to the median of the data set?

   The median is slightly higher (one degree) than the mean. The median is 92°F.

2. Johanna just finished reading five books in five weeks. The five books had these numbers of pages: 208, 250, 163, 420, and 384. If Johanna wants to impress her teacher, which measure of center should Johanna use to report the average number of pages that she read each week?

   She should use the mean number of pages because it is higher than the median. The mean of the data set is 285 and the median is 250.

3. Nafeeza records the number of bagels she sells each day in her bakery for one week.

Day	S	M	T	W	T	F	S
Dozen	24	26	24	27	20	25	38

   What is the range of the data set?

   18

4. Janelle made a line plot that shows the number of siblings the students in her class have. Use the data in the line plot to answer the questions.

   Number of Siblings

   0 1 2 3 4 5 6 7 8 9

   a. What is the median number of siblings?

   1

   b. What is the range of the number of siblings that Janelle's classmates have.

   The range is 6.

Page CC 74

5. Use the data in the dot plot to answer the questions.

   0 1 2 3 4 5 6 7 8 9 10 11 12 13 14 15 16 17 18 19 20

   a. What is the range of scores?

   20 − 16 = 4

   b. What does the range indicate?

   The number of questions answered varies from 16 correct to 20 correct. The scores are clustered together.

   c. What is the median?

   18.5

   d. Is the median a data value? Explain.

   It is not because there are an even number of values and the median falls between two different values.

   e. What is the mean?

   18.3

   f. Does the mean make sense? Explain.

   Sample answer: Yes. Since there are more scores to the right of 18 than to the left of 18, it makes sense that the mean is to the right of 18.

Page CC 75

Name _____

Common Core Standards Practice

6.SP.B.4 Display numerical data in plots on a number line, including dot plots, histograms, and box plots.

1. Mr. Lenz surveyed his friends to determine the number of hours they sleep per night. The data are shown in the table.

6	7	8	6	7	9	5	7
8	4	7	7	5	7	6	8

   a. Create a dot plot of the data.

   4   5   6   7   8   9

   b. Determine the following values and draw a box plot for the data.

   Minimum = **4**   Median = **7**

   Quartile 1 = **6**   Quartile 3 = **7.5**

                            Maximum = **9**

   4   5   6   7   8   9

2. The frequency table below shows the number of hours of battery life for several different cell phones. Draw a histogram of the data.

Hours of Battery Life	Number of Cell Phones
8–10	4
11–13	6
14–16	5
17–19	3

Cell Phone Battery Life

Page CC 76

3. The table shows the total number of home runs hit by the baseball team for the past 10 years.

36	27	23	32	30
27	24	39	63	36

   Determine the following values and draw a box plot for the data.

   Minimum = **23**   Median = **31**

   Quartile 1 = **27**   Quartile 3 = **36**

                            Maximum = **63**

   24 28 32 36 40 44 48 52 56 60 64

4. The Franklin Pottery Company keeps track of the number of broken pieces of pottery per shipment. Draw a histogram of the data.

Number of Broken Pieces	Number of Shipments
0–10	2
11–20	0
21–30	4
31–40	12
41–50	10

Broken Pottery

Common Core Standards Practice

6.SP.B.5ab Summarize numerical data sets in relation to their context, such as by: Reporting the number of observations; Describing the nature of the attribute under investigation, including how it was measured and its units of measurement.

1. Pete's Second Hand Store has several used bicycles for sale. Pete published information about the bicycles in the table shown below.

Used Bicycles for Sale

Inventory number	100	101	102	200	201	202	300	301	302
Condition	OK	OK	fair	good	good	good	very good	very good	like new
Age of bicycle (years)	N/A*	10	9	10	10	N/A*	4	3	1
Wheel diameter (inches)	22	24	24	22	21	22	20	22	24
Price	$12	$15	$18	$30	$30	$30	$85	$85	$150

*Data not available.

For each type of information in the table, write it in each of the columns that describes the type.

Can be Measured with a Tool	Depends on Someone's Judgement	Represents a Fact About a Bicycle
Wheel diameter	Condition, Price	Wheel diameter, Age, Inventory number

page CC 77

---

2. Big City Airlines flies passengers between 6 large U.S. cities. The table shows information about their schedule for the month of June.

Flight Schedule for Big City Airlines

KEY:
606 mi: flight distance
5 flights: number of flights, each way
$250: round trip fare per passenger

	Chicago, IL	Denver, CO	Los Angeles, CA	Minneapolis, MN	New York City, NY
Atlanta, GA	606 mi 5 flights $250	1,199 mi 1 flight $300	1,945 mi 2 flights $400	907 mi 2 flights $280	764 mi 0 flights
Chicago, IL		889 mi 3 flights $200	1,746 mi 2 flights $400	349 mi 5 flights $200	727 mi 5 flights $280
Denver, CO			864 mi 0 flights	677 mi 3 flights $250	1,622 mi 4 flights $400
Los Angeles, CA				1,535 mi 2 flights $350	2,430 mi 4 flights $550
Minneapolis, MN					1,019 mi 3 flights $300

a. How many flights does the airline fly to and from Atlanta? **10 flights**

b. How many flights does the airline fly to and from Los Angeles? **10 flights**

c. Of the three types of data presented in the table, which is a measurement? What is the unit of the measurement?
Flight distance is a measurement. The unit is miles (mi).

d. Which data in the table might change from one month to the next? Explain why these data might change.
The number of flights and the fares could change. The airline might adjust both their flight schedule and fares to increase their business.

page CC 78

Common Core Standards Practice

6.SP.B.5c Summarize numerical data sets in relation to their context, such as by: Giving quantitative measures of center (median and/or mean) and variability (interquartile range and/or mean absolute deviation), as well as describing any overall pattern and any striking deviations from the overall pattern with reference to the context in which the data were gathered.

1. A group of 12 experts each assesses the value of an antique doll. Their estimates are listed in the data table.

$50	$52	$60	$48	$59	$63
$21	$51	$95	$58	$56	$59

a. How do the mean and median of the data set compare?
The median is slightly greater than the mean. The median is 57 and the mean is 56.

b. What is the mean absolute deviation of the data set? What does it tell you about the data set?
$9.67. It indicates how much the different values deviate from the mean.

c. What pattern do you observe in the data? What deviations, if any, do you notice in the pattern?
Most of the data values are between $48 and $63. Two values are striking deviations: one very low ($21) and one very high ($95).

d. The same experts independently assess the value of an antique lamp. These estimates are shown in the table below.

$10	$120	$156	$15	$18	$140
$13	$20	$136	$17	$15	$12

The mean of this data set is $56, which was also the mean of the data set for the doll. How are the two data sets different? Consider both the measures of center and variability.

The data set for the lamp has a much greater variability. The range of the second data set is 146 whereas the range in the first data set is 74. The measures of center for the first data set are close: mean = 56; median = 57. The measures of center for the second data set are spread out: mean = 56; median = 17.5.

page CC 79

---

2. The Fairfield Skyliners played 15 football games this season. The table shows the points they scored in each game.

3	35	10	30	18	45	41	38
21	39	38	14	32	27	30	

a. Why is it useful to list values in order when determining measures of variability?
Sample answer: When a data set is ordered from least to greatest, the interquartile range can be easily determined. The interquartile range is a useful measure of variability.

b. Determine these values for the data set.

Median __30__   Third quartile __38__

First quartile __18__   Interquartile range __20__

c. Describe the pattern of the data.
Sample answer: The values that are less than the median are distributed more widely than the values that are greater than the median.

3. The table shows the number of customers at Julie's Restaurant during one week.

Sunday	Monday	Tuesday	Wednesday	Thursday	Friday	Saturday
290	123	150	159	190	245	390

a. What pattern do you notice in the data?
The restaurant has the most customers on Friday, Saturday, and Sunday. The number of customers increases from Monday to Saturday.

page CC 80

Page CC 81

Name _____

Common Core Standards Practice

6.SP.B.5d Summarize numerical data sets in relation to their context, such as by: Relating the choice of measures of center and variability to the shape of the data distribution and the context in which the data were gathered.

1. Peter and Amy go bowling every Saturday. The table shows their scores from 6 games.

Player	Game 1	Game 2	Game 3	Game 4	Game 5	Game 6
Peter	90	75	82	66	94	67
Amy	79	81	77	79	78	80

a. Of mean, median, and range, which statistic best explains the difference in the shape of Peter's scores and Amy's scores? Explain your answer.

The range of their scores best explains the difference. Both scores are evenly distributed about a similar mean or median, but Peter's scores are distributed across a much larger range.

b. Peter and Amy each won half of the games they played. Is this fact better explained by comparing the means or the ranges of their scores? Explain your answer.

The mean better explains this fact. Because the mean score for both bowlers was the same, it can be predicted that each bowler will win some of the games.

2. Dan and Nancy also bowl every Saturday. The table shows their scores from 6 games.

Player	Game 1	Game 2	Game 3	Game 4	Game 5	Game 6
Dan	83	86	84	50	88	87
Nancy	50	55	57	59	92	52

Compare the shape of Dan's scores with the shape of Nancy's scores. Include the concept of mean or median in your answer.

Both bowlers have one score that is an outlier because it deviates greatly from the mean, while the other scores are much closer to the mean. For Dan, the outlier is lower than the mean. For Nancy, the outlier is higher.

CC 81

page CC 81

Page CC 82

3. A scientist compares two different kinds of grasshoppers. She measures the length of 6 adults from each species. The results are shown in the table.

Species	Length (centimeters)					
A	4.3	4.1	3.9	4.5	4.3	4.2
B	1.4	4.3	2.0	3.9	1.5	2.8

a. A science student finds an adult grasshopper that belongs either to Species A or Species B. She measures its length to be 1.8 cm. Based on the data in the table, can she determine the species? Explain your answer using the terms *mean* or *range*.

Yes, it belongs to Species B. The length is within the wide range of lengths that the table shows for Species B, but not within the narrow range for Species A.

b. A second grasshopper also belongs to either Species A or Species B. Its length is 4.2 cm. Can its species be determined? Explain your answer.

No. A length of 4.2 cm is within the range of both species.

4. The table shows the number of people who live in each house on a road.

6	5	3	4	4	4	5
3	2	2	7	5	4	4

Mean: 4.14   Median: 4   Range: 5

a. A town official thinks there is an error in the data because it is impossible for a fraction of a person to live in a house. Must the data include an error? Explain your answer.

No, the data could be valid. The mean of a data set is a calculated value, so it could be a rational number.

b. For the whole town, the mean number of people per house is also 4.14. Must the range of values for the town also equal 5 people? Explain your answer.

No. It is possible that some houses in town could have more than 7 people while enough houses have fewer than 4 people to keep the mean at 4.14.

CC 82

page CC 82

Page CC 83

Name _____

Practice End-of-Year Assessment

1. a. Write an inequality to compare the numbers −6 and −3.

−6 < −3

b. Plot the two numbers on the number line shown below.

c. Which number is to the left of the other number? Explain why it is to the left.

−6 is to the left of −3 because −6 is the lesser number.

2. b. What is the coefficient of *x* in the expression shown below?

5 + 3x − 4y

3

3. Describe a ratio of 4:1 that occurs in nature.

Possible answers: In a wolf pack or pride of lions, the ratio of legs to animals is 4:1. In a bundle of four-leaf clovers, the ratio of leaves to stems is 4:1.

CC 83

page CC 83

Page CC 84

4. The diagram shows a three-dimensional figure. Its base is a square that measures 4 inches by 4 inches. Its four triangular sides meet at a point that is 6 inches from the midpoint of each side of the square.

Square base
4 in. x 4 in.

a. What is the name of this figure?

square pyramid

b. Draw the net for the figure.

6 in.

4 in.
4 in.

c. Use the net to calculate the surface area of the figure.

64 in.²

CC 84

page CC 84

T21

page CC 85

5. a. What is the distance between the point A and point B shown in the graph?

6 units

b. Tell how you found the distance.

Check students' answers.

6. Explain why the question below is a statistical question.

People leaving a movie are asked, "What did you think of the movie?"

It is a statistical question because there will be variability in the responses.

7. Find the quotient.

$$\frac{3}{2} \div \frac{3}{8}$$

$$\frac{3}{2} \div \frac{3}{8} = \frac{3}{2} \times \frac{8}{3} = \frac{8}{2} = 4$$

8. Draw a box plot for this set of data.

5, 10, 10, 12, 12, 15, 18, 20, 24

---

page CC 86

9. The students in art class are working with small cubes.

The teacher asks each student to assemble the small cubes into a large cube that measures n cubes on each side, with n an integer that each student chooses.

The diagram shows one example of a completed assignment, in which n = 4.

a. How many small cubes are used in the figure shown above? Show how you found the answer.

$$4^3 = 64 \text{ cubes}$$

b. Write an expression for the number of small cubes used in each student's art work as a function of n.

$$n \cdot n \cdot n$$

10. Mr. Brock's bank account is overdrawn by $52. He makes a deposit of $100. Assuming he has made no other withdrawals or deposits, is his account still overdrawn? Explain your answer.

No, he had deposited more than the amount of the overdraft.

---

page CC 87

11. During the first week of July, Simon earned $65.00 for mowing lawns. This amount represents 40 percent of the total amount he earned in July.

a. Write an equation that can be used to determine the total amount T that Simon earned in July.

$$65.00 = 0.40 \times T$$

b. Solve the equation to find T. Explain what your solution means.

162.50

Simon earned $162.50 in July.

12. Simplify the expression below.

$26 - 3 \times 4 + 8 = \square$

22

13. A right rectangular prism is $7\frac{1}{3}$ inches long, $2\frac{1}{2}$ inches wide, and 6 inches tall. What is the volume of the prism?

110 cubic inches

---

page CC 88

14. Describe a real-life use for the expression 12x + 6y.

Possible answers: The expression could show the total revenue from selling x items at $12 each and y items at $6 each. It could show the total number of eggs held in x cartons that hold 12 eggs each plus y cartons that hold 6 eggs each.

15. A cyclist rides a 25-mile stretch of road at a constant speed. It takes her 90 minutes to ride the 25 miles. At what speed is she riding?

16.67 miles per hour

16. What is the greatest common factor of 64 and 80?

16

17. Which expression is equivalent to the expression shown below?

$2 \times (x + y) + 2 \times (x + 1)$

A $2x + 2y + 2$

B $2x + 2y - 2$

Ⓒ $4x + 2y + 2$

D $2y - 2$

18. At closing time, a pizza restaurant has $5\frac{5}{8}$ pizzas still unsold. The manager divides the pizzas equally among the 3 workers to take home.

    a. Draw a model to match the problem situation.

Check students' models.

    b. How much pizza does each worker receive?

Each worker gets $1\frac{7}{8}$ pizza.

19. Plot the following numbers on the number line.

    $-15, 45, -50, 20$

page CC 89

---

20. Alicia and Myron are bowlers. The table shows their scores for 7 games.

Alicia	70	72	74	71	72	72	73
Myron	70	60	85	74	81	65	69

How are the seven scores for each player alike? How are they different? Discuss center and variability in your answer.

The center is the same (or close to the same) for both bowlers. However, Alicia's scores have much less variability. All of her scores were close to the center. Myron's scores varied more.

21. The fare on a railroad is 40 cents for every mile of travel, plus an additional $15. Write an expression for the cost, in dollars, of a trip of n miles.

$0.40n + 15$

22. During one evening, a restaurant used 105 patties to make triple-stack burgers. Each triple-stack burger has 3 patties.

    a. Write an equation that can be used to determine the number of triple-stack burgers the restaurant served that evening.

    $3z = 105$

    b. Solve the equation to find z the number of triple-stack burgers.

    $z = 35$

23. Find the product of 15.48 and 8.19.

126.7812

page CC 90

---

24. Ollie sells soft drinks at a baseball stadium. The graph below shows the relationship between his sales per game and the attendance at the stadium.

According to the graph, how does attendance affect Ollie's sales?

Ollie's sales per game increase as attendance increases to about 10,000 people. When attendance is greater than 10,000 people, Ollie's sales remain at $500 per game.

25. Howard has a flexible pipe that is 3 feet long. He wants to use the pipe to connect a faucet to a water tank. The faucet can be moved, but the water tank is fixed in one place.

    a. How far from the water tank can the faucet be? Write an inequality to represent the possible distances.

    $x \leq 3$

    b. Represent the inequality on the number line shown here.

page CC 91

---

26. a. On the coordinate plane below, plot and label the points with coordinates (3, 4) and (−3, 4).

    b. How do the locations of the two points differ from each other?

    Possible answers: Point (3, 4) is in the first quadrant; point (−3, 4) is in the second quadrant. Point (3, 4) is to the right, or positive side, of the y-axis. Point (−3, 4) is to the left, or negative side, of the y-axis.

27. Workers pick 4,583 melons from a large field. Then they pack them into crates that hold 18 melons each. How many crates do they need to hold all of the melons? Explain your answer.

They will need 255 crates. The last crate will have only 11 melons.

28. Which statement best describes the values of x that make this statement true?

    $|x| < 3$

    A The absolute value of x is greater than 3.
    B The absolute value of x is either 0, 1, or 2.
    C The difference between x and 0 is less than 3.
    D The difference between x and 0 is greater than 3.

page CC 92

29. A trucker is 140 miles away from his destination. To arrive there in $2\frac{1}{2}$ hours, at what constant speed should he travel?

56 miles per hour

30. Which of the following are solutions to the inequality below? Circle all that apply.

$x - 5 < 9$

⑨   15   ⑫

14   18   20

31. What is 1.52 less than 6.8?

5.28

32. At the library, each rack can display 6 magazines. The librarian has 72 magazines to display. How many racks does he need?

a. Write an equation that can be used to determine the number of racks the librarian needs. Use n to represent the number of racks.

$6n = 72$

b. Solve for n.

The librarian needs 12 racks

page CC 93

---

33. Dave buys 50 apples for $28. What is his cost per apple?

$0.56, or 56 cents, per apple

34. Explain why $9(t - 1)$ is equivalent to $9t - 9$.

The distributive property states that you can multiply each addend by the value, so $9(t - 1) = 9t - 9$.

35. Which expression is equivalent to the expression shown below?

$z - 3 - z + z + 3$

A   0

Ⓑ z

C $3z$

D $3z + 3$

page CC 94

---

36. A figure has vertices at the points (3, 2) (3, −4), (1, −4), and (1, 2).

a. Draw the figure on the coordinate plane shown below.

b. Find the width and length of the figure.

Width: **2 units**

Length: **6 units**

37. Jane is taking part in a reading program. The table shows the books she has read so far.

Type of book	Number
Novels	12
History	6
Sports	3

a. What is the ratio of the number of novels to the number of sports books that Jane has read?

4:1

b. Jane reads 3 more books of each type shown in the table. What is the new ratio of novels to sports books?

5:2

page CC 95

---

38. A theater can hold 128 people. For tonight's show, 102 tickets were sold online. The remaining tickets will be sold at the ticket window. Write an inequality that can be used to determine the number of tickets available for sale at the ticket window. Then solve the inequality.

$102 + n \leq 128$

$n \leq 26$

39. Fran owes $2 in library fines, and Sera owes $8 in library fines.

Write an inequality to compare the amounts that Fran and Sera owe. Use negative numbers.

$-8 < -2$, or $-2 > -8$

40. Find the area of the triangle shown below.

7.5 square inches

41. Circle the values of x that make the inequality true. (More than one value may be a correct answer.)

$x^2 < 9$

−4   −3   ⊝2   ⊝1   ⓪   ①   ②   3   4

page CC 96

page CC 97

42. Mr. Saxon has a balance of −$45 in his bank account. Then he deposits $65 into the account. Assuming he has not made any other deposits or withdrawals, is his account balance positive or negative?

positive

43. The bait store sells 40 earthworms for $2.00. What is the price per earthworm?

5 cents per earthworm

44. What is the distance between the points (1,3) and (1,−2)?

5 units

45. There are 18 players on the Boomtown Bees, a professional basketball team. The table lists the ages of each player.

24	24	25	26	30	21	27	23	22
19	24	25	22	21	24	24	24	23

Describe the shape of the age data.

The data is bell-shaped, with most entries bunched in the center and few entries at each extreme.

---

page CC 98

46. The Freyas family studies their electricity bill and the weather report over a span of 2 years. The line graph shows their electricity use as a function of the daily high temperature.

a. When does the family pay the least for electricity?

When the temperature is around 50°F.

b. When does the family pay the most for electricity?

When the temperature is 80°F or greater.

c. From January to March, the daily high temperature gradually increases from 10°F to 50°F. How does the family's electricity bill change during this time?

The bill gradually decreases.

d. From April to July, the daily high temperature gradually increases from 50°F to 80°F. How does the family's electricity bill change during this time?

The bill gradually increases.

---

page CC 99

47. Which of the values below make the equation true? Circle all that apply.

$9 + x = 12$

−4　−3　1　2　③　4

48. What is the value of 4^3?

64

49. The table shows the number of tournament victories this season for the 9 members of the chess team.

13	12	8	6	11	8	5	10	8

How do the mean and median of the data set compare?

The mean is slightly higher than the median. The mean is 9 and the median is 8.

50. Which expression is equivalent to the expression shown below?

$8x − 2(5 − x)$

A　$6x − 10$
Ⓑ　$10x − 10$
C　$7x − 10$
D　$8x − 10$

---

page CC 100

Name _____

Performance Task 1

Band Souvenirs

Part A

The Metal Pipes rock band is about to release a new album and will then go on a 20-city concert tour. They are working with an artist to create a cover for their new album, which they will also use to create T-shirts to sell at each concert venue. The artist is charging the band $2,500 to create a cover.

The band manager has received quotes from two different companies that make custom T-shirts. Both quotes include the cost of the T-shirt and the printing of the logo on it. Custom Print charges $7.50 for each T-shirt. A second company, Prince Printing, has quoted a one-time set up fee of $1,250 and $7.25 per T-shirt.

1. How much will different quantities of T-shirts cost at Custom Print and at Prince Printing? Create a table to show the cost for 2,000, 5,000, and 10,000 T-shirts at each company.

Number of T-shirts	2,000	5,000	10,000
Cost at Custom Print	$15,000	$37,500	$75,000
Cost at Prince Printing	$15,750	$37,500	$73,750

2. Which printer should the band use if they plan to have printed 5,000 T-shirts? Should they use the same printer if they plan to have printed 10,000 T-shirts? Explain your answers.

Sample answer: They could use either Custom Print or Prince Printing if they plan to print 5,000 T-shirts. Both would charge the same amount. If the band wanted to print 10,000 T-shirts, they should use Prince Printing because the cost would be less.

Part B

The band manager places an order for 10,000 T-shirts with the lower-cost printing company. He expects to give away 10% of the T-shirts to promote the band's new album and concert tour and will sell the rest for $15 at each concert venue.

3. How many T-shirts does the band need to sell to cover all of the costs of production?

The band needs to sell 5,084 T-shirt to break even. The total cost of producing the T-shirts is $73,750 + 2,500 = $76,350. If the band sells the T-shirts for $15, they would need to sell 5,084 T-shirts to cover the cost of the production.

4. How much would the band make in profit if they sold all of the T-shirts available for sale? Justify your answers.

The band plans to give away 10% of the T-shirts produced, or 1,000 T-shirts, so they have 9,000 left to sell. Selling them all would net $135,000. After subtracting $76,350 in costs, the band's profit would be $58,650.

page CC 101

Name _____

Performance Task 2
Recruiting a Running Back

Part A

Roy and Kwame are running backs at two rival high schools in the same football league. In the table at the right are the number of yards gained per game by each of these two players during the football season.

At the end of the season, awards are given to the outstanding players in the league. Both Roy and Kwame have been nominated to win the award for best running back. The award for best running back is based on the player's game statistics.

Yards Gained per Game	
Roy	Kwame
97	84
68	95
125	107
188	101
116	115
85	91
45	105
108	83
146	93
60	112
118	110
92	104

1. Which player should receive the award for the Best Running Back of the Year for the league based on his game statistics? Justify your answer using measures of center (mean and median) for each player.

Sample answer: Roy should win the award for the league's Best Running Back of the Year, considering the measures of center for both Roy's and Kwame's game statistics. Both had the same median yardage per game, but Roy had a slightly higher mean yardage per game.

Roy:

median $= \frac{(97 + 108)}{2} = \frac{102.5 \text{ yd}}{\text{game}}$

mean $= \frac{1,248}{12} = \frac{104 \text{ yd}}{\text{game}}$

Kwame:

median $= \frac{(101 + 104)}{2} = \frac{102.5 \text{ yd}}{\text{game}}$

mean $= \frac{1,200}{12} = \frac{100 \text{ yd}}{\text{game}}$

page CC 102

Part B

A college recruiter wants to offer a football scholarship to one of the two running backs. When the recruiter looks at a running back's game statistics, he looks for consistency in performance as well as the mean number of yards gained. Consistency means less variability in the data. The recruiter looks at the measures of variability for each player.

2. Based on the data in the table in Part A, who should the recruiter choose, Roy or Kwame? Justify your answer using a measure of variability, either interquartile range and mean absolute deviation. Explain your choice of measure of variability.

Based on the data in the table, the recruiter should offer a football scholarship to Kwame. Even though Roy had a greater mean yardage per game, Kwame was a more consistent player, because there is less variability in his data based on either the interquartile range or the mean absolute deviation of each data set.

Roy:

first quartile: $76.5 \left[\frac{(68 + 85)}{2}\right]$

third quartile:

$121.5 \left[\frac{(118 + 125)}{2}\right]$

Roy's interquartile range: $121.5 - 76.5 = 45$

Kwame:

first quartile: $92 \left[\frac{(91 + 93)}{2}\right]$

third quartile:

$108.5 \left[\frac{(107 + 110)}{2}\right]$

Kwame's interquartile range: $108.5 - 92 = 16.5$.

The data show that Kwame is a much more consistent player than Roy, whose data show much more variability.

The Mean Absolute Deviation also shows less variability in Kwame's statistics.

The mean absolute deviation for Roy's data set:
$(59 + 44 + 36 + 19 + 12 + 7 + 4 + 12 + 14 + 21 + 42 + 84) \div 12 = 354 \div 12 = 29.5$

The mean absolute deviation for Kwame's data set:
mean absolute deviation $= (17 + 16 + 9 + 7 + 5 + 1 + 4 + 5 + 7 + 10 + 12 + 15) \div 12 = 108 \div 12 = 9$

page CC 103

Name _____

Practice End-of-Year Assessment
Test 2

1. a. Write an inequality to compare the numbers −4 and −1.

$$-4 < -1$$

b. Plot the two numbers on the number line shown below.

c. Which number is to the left of the other number? Explain why it is to the left.

−4 is to the left of −1 because −4 is the lesser number.

2. What is the coefficient of x in the expression shown below?

$12 − 2x + 8y$

−2

3. Walter is studying the automobiles in the school parking lot. Describe a ratio of 4:1 that might apply to his observations.

Possible answers: The ratio of number of wheels to the number of automobiles is 4:1.

page CC 105

---

4. The figure below has a circular top and bottom. The circles both have a radius that measures 6 cm. The distance between the two circles is 8 cm.

a. What is the name of this figure?

cylinder

b. Draw the net for the figure.

12π cm
8 cm
6 cm

c. Use the net to calculate the surface area of the figure.

168π cm^2 = about 527.52 cm^2

5. a. What is the distance between the two points shown in the graph?

5 units

(−1, 2)   (4, 2)

b. Tell how you find the distance.

Check students' explanations.

page CC 106

---

6. Explain why the question below is not a statistical question.
People leaving a concert were asked, "What time did the concert end?"

It is not a statistical question because there will not be variability in the responses.

7. Find the quotient.

$\frac{7}{3} \div \frac{3}{4}$

$3\frac{1}{9}$

8. The students in Mrs. Otis's class took a math test. The table shows their scores. Draw a histogram for this set of data.

74	86	65	95	97	100	77	89	94
67	77	88	78	81	84	69	79	87

page CC 107

---

9. Students are working with small cubes. The teacher asks each student to assemble the cubes in a prism that measures s cubes on each side of the base and s cubes along the height. Each student chooses an integer s.

The diagram shows one example of a completed assignment, in which $s = 3$.

a. How many small cubes are used in the figure shown above? Show how you found the answer.

3^3 = 27 cubes

b. Write an expression for the number of small cubes used in each student's prism in terms of s.

$n \cdot n \cdot n$

10. Dr. Kane's bank account is overdrawn by $42. She makes three deposits of $50 each. Assuming she has not made other withdrawals or deposits, is her account still overdrawn? Explain your answer.

No, she had deposited more than the amount of the overdraft.

page CC 108

11. A dirt path leads from the highway to the Carmona ranch. Mrs. Carmona wants to pave 720 feet of the path, a length that is 60% of the total length.

    a. Write an equation that includes L, the total length of the dirt path.

$$720 = 0.60 \times L$$

    b. Solve the equation to find L.

The length of the path is 1,200 feet.

12. Simplify the expression below.

$8 + 2 \times 9 \times 3 - 2 \times 5 = \boxed{}$

52

13. A right rectangular prism is $5\frac{1}{3}$ inches long, $4\frac{1}{2}$ inches wide, and 8 inches tall. What is the volume of the prism?

192 cubic inches

page CC 109

14. Describe a real-life use for the expression $3x + 2y$.

Possible answers: The expression could show the total revenue from selling x items at \$3 each and y items at \$2 each. At a basketball game, it could show the total number of points from x long goals (worth 3 points each) and y short goals (worth 2 points each.)

15. A toy car travels 15 meters at a constant speed. Its travel time is 2.5 minutes. What is the speed of the toy car?

6 meters/minute

16. What is the least common multiple of 9 and 12?

36

page CC 110

17. Which expression is equivalent to the expression shown below?

$(x + y) + 4 \times (x - 1) - y$

    A $4x - 4$
    B $5x + y - 4$
    C $4x + 2y$
    Ⓓ $5x - 4$

18. The supermarket receives cereal boxes in large crates. The boxes in each crate will fill $1\frac{3}{4}$ shelves in the cereal aisle. How many crates are needed to fill 4 empty shelves?

    a. Draw a model to match the problem situation.

Check students' models.

    b. How many crates are needed to fill 4 empty shelves?

7 crates

19. Plot the following numbers on the number line.

50, −25

page CC 111

20. Benji and Chloe play miniature golf. The table shows their scores for 7 games.

Benji	30	32	31	32	30	31	31
Chloe	25	36	31	27	34	30	34

How are the seven scores for each player alike? How are they different? Discuss center and variability in your answer.

The center is the same for both Benji and Chloe. Benji's scores have much less variability. All of his scores are within 1 of the mean. Chloe's scores were as much as 6 away from the mean.

21. On Bonanza Airlines, the fee to check a suitcase is 20 cents for every pound, plus an additional \$5. Write an expression for the fee, in dollars, to check a suitcase that weighs n pounds.

$0.20n + 5$

22. Jessie earns \$9 per hour for babysitting her neighbor's kids. She earned \$162 babysitting last month.

    a. Write an equation that includes h, the number of hours she babysat last month.

$9h = 162$

    b. Solve the equation to find h.

$h = 18$

page CC 112

23. Find the quotient.

$367.72 \div 14.5$

25.36

24. On a TV quiz show, a team has 10 seconds to answer a question. If the team answers correctly, they receive a number of points that varies with the time, as shown in the graph.

Describe the relationship between the time that a team takes to answer the question and the points that they receive.

During the first 5 seconds, the points for a correct answer decrease from 400 to 200. After the first 5 seconds, a correct answer earns 200 points.

25. To win a trophy from the skating club, a skater must earn at least 4 points in the annual tournament.

a. Write an inequality to show the possible number of points that will win the skater a trophy. Use x to represent the number of points earned in the annual tournament.

$x \geq 4$

b. Represent the inequality on the number line shown here.

page CC 113

---

26. a. On the coordinate plane shown below, label the points with coordinates (2,3) and (−2,3).

b. How do the locations of the two points differ from each other?

Possible answers: Point (2,3) is in the first quadrant; point (−2,3) is in the second quadrant. Point (2,3) is to the right, or positive side, of the y-axis. Point (−2,3) is to the left, or negative side, of the y-axis.

27. Workers pick 1,573 apples from a large orchard. Then they pack them into barrels that hold 36 apples each. How many barrels do they need to hold all of the apples? Explain your answer.

1,573 ÷ 36 = 43 R25

Because the 25 apples must fit into a barrel, they need 44 barrels.

28. Which statement best describes the values of x that make this statement true?

$|x| > 9$

A x is greater than 9.

B x is less than −9.

C The difference between the absolute value of x and 0 is less than or equal to 9.

D The difference between the absolute value of x and 0 is greater than 9.

page CC 114

---

29. A trucker is 210 miles away from his destination. To arrive there in $3\frac{1}{2}$ hours, at what constant speed should she travel?

60 miles per hour

30. Which of the following are solutions to the inequality below? Circle all that apply.

$x + 3 < 5$

2   5   8   3   9

①   ⓪   7   10

31. Find the sum of 8.8 and 9.52.

18.32

32. Drew has determined that she needs to keep 7 hens for every rooster on her farm. Today she counted 84 hens.

a. Write an equation that can be used to determine the number of roosters that Drew needs to have on her farm. Use n to represent the number of roosters.

$7n = 84$

b. Solve for n.

Drew should have 12 roosters.

page CC 115

---

33. José buys 50 sports cards for $4.50. What is his cost per card?

$.09, or 9 cents, per card

34. Which expression is equivalent to the expression shown below?

$10k - 9 - 6k + 10$

A $4k + 1$

B $9 - 6k$

C $20k - 15$

D $k + 4$

35. Which expression is equivalent to the expression shown below?

$q - 7 - q - q + 10$

A 3

B $3q$

C $3 - q$

D $q - 3$

page CC 116

36. A polygon has vertices at the points $(-3,-1)$, $(5,-1)$, $(-3,-4)$ and $(5,-4)$.

a. Draw the figure on the coordinate plane shown below.

b. Find the width and length of the figure.

Width: **8 units**

Length: **3 units**

37. Juan, a musician, plays 16 songs at a concert. The chart shows the number of each type of song.

Type of song	Number
Rock-and-roll	8
Country-western	6
Classical	2

a. What is the ratio of the number of rock-and-roll songs to the number of country-western songs that Juan plays?

4:3

b. At the next concert, Juan adds 6 more songs to increase the total to 22 songs. He adds two of each type of song listed in the table. What is the new ratio of rock-and-roll songs to country-western songs?

5:4

page CC 117

---

38. At the aquarium, the guppy tank has enough room for 85 guppies. The tank currently holds 73 guppies. What is the maximum number of guppies that the keeper can add to the tank? Write an inequality that can be used to determine the number of guppies that can be added to the tank. Then solve the inequality.

$$73 + n \le 85$$

$$n \le 12$$

39. On Tuesday at noon, the temperature in Barrow, Alaska, was $-16°C$. The next day at noon, the temperature was $-19°C$.

Write an inequality to compare the two temperatures.

$$-19°C < -16°C, \text{ or } -16°C > -19°C$$

40. Find the area of the parallelogram shown below.

15 square inches

41. For the inequality shown below, circle the values of x that make the inequality true. (More than one value may be a correct answer.)

$x^2 \ge 9$

(-4)   (-3)   -2   -1   0   1   2   (3) (4)

page CC 118

---

42. Ms. Piper has a balance of $-\$35$ in her bank account. Then she deposits $\$76$ into the account. Assuming she has not made any other deposits or withdrawals, is her account balance positive or negative? Explain how you know.

positive; check students' explanations.

43. The bait store sells 25 minnows for $\$4.00$. What is the price per minnow?

16 cents per minnow

44. What is the distance between the points $(3,5)$ and $(3,-2)$? Explain how you know.

7 units; check students' explanations.

45. Nine players on the high school basketball team scored points in their most recent game. The table lists the number of points that each player scored.

11	11	8	5	3	2	2	2	1

Describe the shape of the data.

The data is bimodal with peaks at the left and the right, but few points in the middle.

page CC 119

---

46. During recess at Fern Hill School, the children may choose to play outdoors or in the gym. The graph shows the average number of children who play outdoors as a function of the temperature.

a. When do the greatest number of children choose to play outdoors?

When the temperature is between 40°F and 70°F.

b. When do the fewest children choose to play outdoors?

When the temperature is below 20°F or above 90°F.

c. From January to March, the temperature at recess gradually increases from 20°F to 40°F. How does the number of children who play outdoors change during this time?

An increasing number of children choose to play outdoors.

d. From April to June, the temperature at recess gradually increases from 40°F to 70°F. How does the number of children who play outdoors change during this time?

The number of children who play outdoors stays about the same.

page CC 120

47. Which of the values below make the equation true? Circle all that apply

$2x + 8 = 20$

−6   4   2   (6)   8

48. What is the value of the expression $3^3 − 1$?

26

49. The table shows the number of tournament victories this season for the 9 members of the chess team. The mean number of victories is 8.

Number of victories	12	11	7	5	10	7	4	8	8
Deviation from mean	4	3	1	3	2	1	4	0	0

What is the mean absolute deviation of the data set? What does the mean absolute deviation tell you about the data?

2; The mean absolute deviation says that on average the number of victories is between two more and two less than 8.

50. Which expression is equivalent to the expression shown below?

$4x + 3(5 + x)$

A $3x + 15$
B $x + 15$
C $7x + 15$
D $3x + 5$

page CC 121

Name _____

Performance Task 3
Stadium Seats
Part A

The 4,250 seats at a high school football stadium need to be painted. The high school business manager received paint and labor estimates from two different painting crews.

Michael's Painting Crew Painting Proposal	Date	Proposal No.	Sales Rep.
	Sep 8	613	Robin

Materials

Quantity	Description	Unit Price	Total
20	Primer paint	$20.99	$410.20
40	Latex outdoor paint	$22.99	$919.60

Labor

Quantity	Description	Unit Price	Total
215	Labor	$45.00	$9,675.00

ProPainting Crew Painting Proposal	Date	Proposal No.	Sales Rep.
	September 10	122	Al

Quantity	Description	Unit Price	Total
4,250	Power washing to remove dirt and mildew	$0.35	$1,487.50
4,250	Primer coat	$0.75	$3,187.50
4,250	Two coats, latex paint	$1.50	$6,375.00

Prices quoted include all materials and labor.

1. How do the costs per seat compare between the two proposals? Tell how you determined your answer.

The two proposals have very similar costs-per-seat, with Michael's Painting Crew having a slightly lower cost-per-seat: $2.59 compared to ProPainting Crew's cost-per-seat of $2.60.

page CC 122

---

2. Which painting crew should the manager hire to do the work? Give at least two reasons to support your answer.

Check students' recommendation and supporting arguments. Considerations: ProPainting's proposal looks more comprehensive, but Michael's proposal is less expensive.

Part B

The business manager is told that the work needs to be done for the first home game of the football season, in less than two weeks. Both painting companies said they would have to add a surcharge to get the work done that quickly. Michael's Painting Crew will add a 25% surcharge to the cost of labor, while ProPainting Crew will add a 10% surcharge to total cost.

3. Which painting crew would you now recommend the manager hire to do the work? Give at least two reasons to support your answer.

Check students' recommendation and supporting arguments. Considerations: even with the 25% surcharge on labor, Michael's proposal is still less expensive ($12,093.75 vs $12,155). On the other hand, ProPainting's proposal may still seem to be more comprehensive as it specifies that the seats will be power washed and that 2 coats of paint will be applied to each seat.

page CC 123

Name _____

Performance Task 4
Making Towels
Part A

Mr. Angler has been contracted to make towels for the Northwoods Resort. He will make 50 hand towels, 50 bath towels, and 35 beach towels. The dimensions for each type of towel are shown in the table below.

Type of Towel	Dimensions
Hand	1 ft × $1\frac{7}{8}$ ft
Bath	$2\frac{1}{4}$ ft × $4\frac{1}{2}$ ft
Beach	3 ft × $5\frac{3}{4}$ ft

Mr. Angler will use the same terry cloth material for the hand towels and bath towels. He can get 50 yards of cloth for a very good price, which will increase his profit for this contract. The cloth is 60 inches wide.

1. Will Mr. Angler be able to make 50 hand towels and 50 bath towels with the 50 yards of cloth? If so, how much cloth will remain? If not, how much more cloth will he need?

Yes, he can make the 100 towels with the 50 yards. He'll need $43\frac{3}{4}$ yards of cloth, with $6\frac{1}{4}$ yards remaining. He can cut 5 hand towels on the width of the cloth (60 inches). Each of the five towels will require $1\frac{7}{8}$ ft or $22\frac{1}{2}$ inches, for a total of 225 inches or $6\frac{1}{4}$ yards. For the bath towels, he can either cut two across the width (27 in 2 = 54 in) and use 54 inches of length × 25, or one across the width (54 inches) and 27 inches of length × 50, for a total of 1,350 inches or $37\frac{1}{2}$ yards.

page CC 124

Part B

Mr. Angler will use a less expensive terry cloth to make the beach towels. The cloth for the beach towels costs $7 per yard. It is also 60 inches wide. The cloth is sold only by the yard.

2. How much will the terry cloth for beach towels cost Mr. Angler?

The length of the beach towel (69 in.) is greater than the width of the cloth (60 in.), so he will have to place the width of the beach towel (36 in.) along the width of the cloth. He will need 35 lengths of the beach towel, or 69" × 35 = 2,415 inches or $67\frac{1}{12}$ yards. Because the cloth is sold only by the yard, he will need to buy 68 yards for a cost of $476.

page CC 125

Practice End-of-Year Assessments Correlation Chart
Test 1 and Test 2

The chart below provides information about the two Practice End-of-Year Assessments, Test 1, found in the students' workbook and Test 2, a secure version, found in this Teacher's Guide, starting on page CC 105. The chart lists the Standard for Mathematical Content that is the primary assessment focus of each item. It also indicates whether the standard assessed is a major, supporting or additional content emphasis (as determined by both PARCC and SBAC). Finally, the last column points to the lesson(s) in enVisionMATH Common Core where students can be directed if they need additional practice or review of concepts.

Item Test 1 and Test 2	CCSS	Content Emphasis	enVisionMATH Common Core Lessons
1	6.NS.C.7	Major	10-1, 10-2, 10-3
2	6.EE.A.2	Major	2-1
3	6.RP.A.1	Major	12-1
4	6.G.A.4	Supporting	18-1, 18-2, 18-5
5	6.NS.C.8	Major	10-9, 10-10
6	6.SP.A.1	Additional	19-1
7	6.NS.A.1	Major	9-1, 9-3, 9-4
8	6.SP.B.4	Additional	19-6
9	6.EE.A.1	Supporting	1-3
10	6.NS.C.5	Supporting	10-1
11	6.RP.A.3	Major	14-4, 14-5, 14-6
12	6.EE.A.2	Additional	2-3, 2-5, 2-6
13	6.G.A.2	Major	18-3, 18-4
14	6.EE.B.6	Supporting	2-1
15	6.RP.A.3	Major	12-5, 13-2
16	6.NS.B.4	Major	5-2, 5-3
17	6.EE.A.4	Major	4-1
18	6.NS.A.1	Supporting	9-1, 9-3, 9-4, 9-5
19	6.NS.C.6	Major	10-1, 10-2, 10-3
20	6.SP.A.3	Major	19-7

T33

Item Test 1 and Test 2	CCSS	Content Emphasis	enVisionMATH Common Core Lessons
21	6.EE.B.6	Major	2-1
22	6.EE.B.7	Additional	4-4, 4-5
23	6.NS.B.3	Major	3-3, 3-4
24	6.EE.C.9	Major	15-4, 15-5
25	6.EE.B.8	Major	15-6
26	6.NS.C.6	Supporting	10-1, 10-3, 10-9
27	6.NS.B.2	Major	2-6, 3-5
28	6.NS.C.7	Major	10-2, 10-8
29	6.RP.A.3	Major	12-5, 13-2
30	6.EE.B.8	Additional	15-6
31	6.NS.B.3	Supporting	3-1, 3-2
32	6.EE.B.7	Major	4-4, 4-5
33	6.RP.A.2	Major	12-3, 13-2
34	6.EE.A.3	Major	2-2, 2-3, 2-6
35	6.EE.A.4	Major	4-1
36	6.G.A.3	Supporting	10-10, 11-1
37	6.RP.A.1	Supporting	12-1
38	6.EE.B.8	Major	15-6
39	6.NS.C.7	Major	10-1, 10-2
40	6.G.A.1	Major	11-4
41	6.EE.B.5	Major	3-9, 15-6, 15-7
42	6.NS.C.5	Major	10-1
43	6.RP.A.2	Major	12-3, 13-2
44	6.NS.C.8	Major	10-5, 10-9, 10-10
45	6.SP.A.2	Major	19-2
46	6.EE.C.9	Major	15-2, 15-3, 15-4
47	6.EE.B.5	Major	3-9, 4-2
48	6.EE.A.1	Major	1-3
49	6.SP.B.5	Major	19-3, 19-4
50	6.EE.A.3	Major	2-2, 2-4, 4-1

Performance Tasks Scoring Rubrics

Performance Task 1 – Band Souvenirs

Primary Content Domains and Clusters

Ratios and Proportional Relationships: Understand ratio concepts and use ratio reasoning to solve problems. (6.RP.A.2, 6.RP.A.3)

Secondary Content Domains and Clusters

The Number System: Apply and extend previous understandings of multiplication and division to divide fractions by fractions. (6.NS.B.2); Compute fluently with multi-digit numbers and find common factors and multiples. (6.NS.B.3)

Math Practices Focus

MP 1, 2, 3, 4, 7

Scoring Rubric

1	**Creates a table accurately comparing the prices.**	5
	Calculates the cost for each number of T-shirts at each company.	
	Makes an organized table showing all of the data.	
2	**Justifies the correct answer to both questions.**	5
	Answers both questions accurately.	
	Explains why one company is cheaper for 5000 T-shirts while the other is cheaper for 10,000 T-shirts.	
3	**Identifies the number of T-shirts that need to be sold to cover costs.**	5
	Calculates the correct number of T-shirts to break even.	
4	**Determines the profit when selling all the T-shirts.**	5
	Calculates the correct income, costs, and profit.	
	Justifies the profit calculated including all costs and income.	
TOTAL		**20**

Performance Task 2 – Recruiting a Running Back

Primary Content Domains and Clusters

Statistics and Probability: Develop understanding of statistical variability. (6.SP.A.3); Summarize and describe distributions. (6.SP.B.5)

Secondary Content Domains and Clusters

The Number System: Compute fluently with multi-digit numbers and find common factors and multiples. (6.NS.B.3)

Math Practices Focus

MP 1, 2, 3, 6, 7

Scoring Rubric

1	**Selects a measure of center and justifies the choice.**	10
	Calculates measures of center for both players.	
	Compares measures of center.	
	Explains why one player may be the better choice given the player's variability.	
2	**Selects a measure of variability and justifies the choice.**	10
	Calculates measures of variability for both players.	
	Compares measures of variability.	
	Explains why one player may be the better choice given the player's variability.	
TOTAL		20

Performance Task 3 – Stadium Seats

Primary Content Domains and Clusters

Ratios and Proportional Relationships: Understand ratio concepts and use ratio reasoning to solve problems. (6.RP.A.2, 6.RP.A.3)

Secondary Content Domains and Clusters

The Number System: Compute fluently with multi-digit numbers and find common factors and multiples. (6.NS.B.3)

Math Practices Focus

MP 1, 2, 3, 4, 7

Scoring Rubric

1	**Compares unit rates appropriately.**	6
	Calculates the unit rate for each company.	
	Explains the calculation for each unit rate.	
2	**Selects one company and justifies selection.**	4
	Selects one of the two companies.	
	Identifies two factors that make the company preferable.	
3	**Selects one company and justifies selection.**	10
	Calculates total cost after surcharge for each company.	
	Selects one of the two companies.	
	Identifies two factors that make the company preferable.	
TOTAL		20

Performance Task 4 – Making Towels

Primary Content Domains and Clusters

The Number System: Solve real-world and mathematical problems involving area, surface area, and volume. (6.G.A.1)

Number and Operations – Fractions: Apply and extend previous understandings of multiplication and division to multiply and divide fractions. (5.NF.B.6)

Secondary Content Domains and Clusters

Measurement and Data: Convert like measurement units within a given measurement system. (5.MD.A.1)

Math Practices Focus

MP 1, 2, 3, 6, 7

Scoring Rubric

1	Determines the amount of cloth remaining.	10
	Calculate the amount of material needed for the 100 towels.	
	Identify an orientation of the towels from the cloth.	
	Calculate the amount of cloth remaining.	
	Convert units correctly.	
2	Calculates the cost of the cloth for the beach towels.	10
	Identify an orientation of the towels from the cloth.	
	Calculate the length of cloth needed for 35 towels.	
	Convert units correctly.	
	Calculate cost at given rate per yard.	
TOTAL		20